Authors of **Banned Books**

John Steinbeck

Banned, Challenged, and Censored

Maurene J. Hinds

Enslow Publishers, Inc.
40 Industrial Road
Box 398
Berkeley Heights, NJ 07922
USA

http://www.enslow.com

Library of Congress Cataloging-in-Publication Data

Hinds, Maurene J.
  John Steinbeck : banned, challenged, and censored / Maurene J. Hinds.
    p. cm. — (Authors of banned books)
  Includes bibliographical references and index.
  ISBN-13: 978-0-7660-2688-9
  ISBN-10: 0-7660-2688-4
  1. Steinbeck, John, 1902–1968—Criticism and interpretation—Juvenile literature. 2. Steinbeck, John, 1902–1968—Censorship—Juvenile literature. 3. Challenged books—Juvenile literature. 4. Prohibited books—Juvenile literature. 5. Censorship—Juvenile literature. I. Title.
  PS3537.T3234Z7143 2008
  813'.52—dc22

                                                                    2007011686
Printed in the United States of America

10 9 8 7 6 5 4 3 2 1

To Our Readers: We have done our best to make sure that all Internet addresses in this book were active and appropriate when we went to press. However, the author and publisher have no control over and assume no liability for the material available on those Internet sites or on other Web sites they may link to. Any comments or suggestions can be sent by e-mail to comments@enslow.com or to the address on the back cover.

Photo Credits: AP/Wide World, p. 120; Library of Congress, pp. 26, 50, 67, 76, 91, 100, 110, back cover; NOAA Photo Library, p. 34; Office for Intellectual Freedom, American Library Association, p. 129; Pat Hathaway Collection/California Views, pp. 1, 40; Shutterstock, pp. 4, 16, 133.

Cover Photo: Pat Hathaway Collection/California Views.

Contents

Chapter 1

John Steinbeck: A History of Censorship

In 1986, a letter from a grandmother of a Panama City, Florida, student started a chain reaction resulting in two schools, banning more than sixty books. Authors of these books included writers such as William Shakespeare, Ernest Hemingway, Charles Dickens, and Mark Twain. John Steinbeck wrote two of the banned books: *Of Mice and Men* and *The Pearl*.

It started when an English teacher wanted to use *I Am the Cheese*, a book by Robert Cormier, in an advanced class. She sent letters to the students' parents, asking them to sign a permission slip allowing their child to read the book. Students whose parents did not approve of the book could read an alternate book.

Eighty-eight parents approved the book, and four did not.

One student's grandmother wrote a letter of complaint to Bay County School District superintendent Leonard Hall. She expressed concerns about vulgar language and ideas in *I Am the Cheese*. Her daughter, the student's mother, filed a formal complaint. She worried that other students would tease her daughter for not reading the Cormier book. Following the complaints, the teacher was not allowed to use the book in class until a district committee could review the matter. Within a month, that committee approved the use of the book.

Superintendent Hall did not follow the committee's recommendation to use the book. Further, before a public meeting to discuss the issue, he instructed teachers not to discuss the First Amendment, which guarantees free speech, in class. He also instructed teachers to tell the students not to attend the meeting. About three hundred parents attended the meeting. Of those, about a third supported the superintendent's position.[1] At the meeting, Hall argued that the school had not officially accepted the book for use in the classroom. He later expressed personal opinions about the book. He worried that students might distrust the government if they read the book.

Shortly after the public meeting, Hall rejected the use of *I Am the Cheese*, despite most parents' support of the book and the committee's recommendation. He then outlined a five-step process to approve new books.

6

He said that all books not yet approved, aside from textbooks, would go through this process. Hall's plan included the following:

1. Teachers would submit a detailed plan showing what books they wanted to use and why.

2. The principals would either reject the plan or send it to the county instructional staff for review and approval.

3. The county instructional staff would either reject the plan or send it to the superintendent for review and approval.

4. The superintendent would either reject the plan or send it to the school board for review and approval.

5. The school board would make the final decision.[2]

Many people opposed this new rule, feeling that it gave Hall too much control.[3]

The debate over books in the classroom continued for several months. The issue was discussed at another school board meeting. Twenty-five citizens attended the meeting, and seventeen of those argued against Hall's plan. One of the attendees, a former school board member, presented a pile of antiobscenity petitions. He said the petitions included 9,000 signatures. (A journalist later discovered there were 3,549 signatures.)[4] Even so, the school board approved the policy. Hall later added new rules that required teachers to place books in categories according to the amount of obscenity in them. Despite the teacher's attempts to have *I Am the Cheese* and other books approved, students at the school never read the book in the classroom. When it was over, Hall had banned sixty-four titles from use in Bay County schools.[5]

In May 1987, a number of students and parents filed a suit against the school board. They claimed that the strict policy violated the students' First Amendment rights to "receive information and be educated according to their parents' wishes and denied teachers their rights of free speech and academic freedom," as summarized by writer Nicholas J. Karolides.[6] The court decision did not clearly resolve the issue. Then, after Hall decided not to run for superintendent again, a new policy was created with the help of the organization People for the American Way. It was satisfactory to both teachers and the school board.

Although this particular case started with a book by Robert Cormier, the process has been similar for some books by the famous American writer John Steinbeck. Many of his books have been challenged in the school system or banned altogether because of profanity or obscene language. In fact, this has been going on since the books were published and continues today.

Banning Steinbeck

Of Mice and Men is one of the books most often banned or challenged in this country. It has consistently been among the top one hundred most frequently banned books, often listed in the top ten. Another of Steinbeck's books, *The Grapes of Wrath*, is also a frequent target. Immediately after its publication, various people and organizations opposed the book for its content, and the book has been challenged or banned repeatedly ever since, even into the early 2000s.

As recently as 2003, a family at Community High School in Normal, Illinois, complained about *Of Mice and Men*, saying that it has "racial slurs, profanity, violence, and does not represent traditional values."[7] They wanted the book removed but were ultimately unsuccessful. Another book by Steinbeck, *The Pearl,* was offered as an alternate book, but the family turned it down.

After two new members joined the George County, Mississippi, school board in 2002, it banned *Of Mice and Men*. At the time, the book was required reading for an advanced tenth grade English class because it is considered an American classic. The board gave the book's profanity as its reason for the ban; Larry McDonald, one of the new school board members, told the press that the language in *Of Mice and Men* made him uncomfortable.[8] The same year, a school in Grandville, Michigan, challenged the book because of racism, foul language, and profanity.[9]

Many challenges of Steinbeck's books have occurred in addition to these mentioned. What this means is that he is a controversial author. Scholars continue to debate his place in American literature; however, his works are generally considered classics. In 1962, he won the most prestigious award in literature, the Nobel Prize, for his body of work. It seems natural, then, that his books would be taught in English and literature classes. Many high schools use his works, especially *Of Mice and Men* and *The Grapes of Wrath*. Both books were best sellers. Both books received critical praise, although many people consider *The Grapes of Wrath* to be his best work. Steinbeck experimented with form in both books, which makes them a common choice for literary studies. He also dealt with important social issues such as racism, sexism, religion, and social class.

What then, specifically, makes the books so objectionable? Language is one of the primary reasons that people object to the books. Racism and other issues such as sexuality also play a part in the controversy, but obscene language is a recurring theme in arguments against the books.

Steinbeck had an interest in humanity. He attempted to portray people the way they were, not the way people wished they were. Both of these titles deal with working people. Some might call them lower class. In researching the books, Steinbeck interviewed real people. The language used in the books reflects the language he heard in those interviews.

Steinbeck also had an interest in portraying situations without passing judgment on them. He wrote about what was, but did not always answer questions about why things were the way they were. This, too, is reflected in the ideas and language used in his writing. He sought to portray a situation; he left it to readers to make any judgments.

Finally, he aimed to push his craft further. Despite his successes, he did not feel that he had "arrived" at a writing destination. He expected more from himself, and he continued to work toward expanding his writing skills.

Steinbeck was a very private person. He did not enjoy fame, and he did not give many personal interviews. Even though he felt that his works should be viewed on their own merit, people speculated about the writer behind the books. They made assumptions about him, oftentimes incorrect ones—that he was immoral or had certain political beliefs. This may have contributed to early perceptions or issues about his work. While the public and critics often praised his work, it came under fire at times. In addition to attacking his work, some critics made personal attacks on Steinbeck, such as claiming that he was anti-American or a Communist or did not support his home state's agriculture business.

Steinbeck's work continues to be challenged and banned on a consistent basis. Does "bad" language equal a "bad" book? Is language a reason to ban a book? Is it possible to look beyond the language to a deeper understanding of the work? At what age can a reader handle profanity and see the story behind the words? People often ask these questions when challenging or defending a book. They are not easy to answer.

Chapter 2

Book Battles: Book Challenging, Book Banning, and Censorship

Censorship is the practice of removing something that a person or group of people decides is objectionable or unsuitable for another person or group. It can involve things that people say, hear, read, or do. Censorship can happen in large or small settings. These can range from a government censoring information for society to a school censoring information for its students to parents censoring information for their children.

Jethro K. Lieberman, associate dean for academic affairs and professor at New York Law School, writes that there are four kinds of censorship: moral, military, political, and religious.[1] Moral censorship is the most common type, and it relates to a society's, group's, or person's values. Military censorship occurs when information is suppressed that could put a country or its military forces in danger (such as war plans during conflict). Political censorship happens when a government

12

does not want people to have access to some information. This type of censorship usually occurs in nondemocratic countries, such as dictatorships. Finally, religious censorship occurs when certain types of religious expression are not allowed.[2]

Historical Perspective

The practice of censorship dates far back in history. The Romans and Greeks both practiced censorship. One of the most famous historical cases of censorship is that of the philosopher Socrates. He spoke about ideas that the Greeks considered dangerous to youth. His ideas challenged the religious beliefs and the government's policies of the time. Socrates' words and actions angered some people because he challenged the moral and intellectual traits of his peers.[3] In 339 B.C., the people of Athens condemned him to death. Socrates died for speaking out about his beliefs. This may be an extreme example of censorship. However, it shows that censorship has a long history. The people of Athens were not the first, nor the last, to censor their citizens. Nearly all cultures have had or still have some type of censorship laws. Even in the United States, some speech is illegal. This can include using profanity in public or threatening to harm the president.

Book banning also has a long history. It has taken place since the earliest forms of printing—especially with Gutenberg's invention of a printing press with movable type in 1450. In the United States, there have been debates over free speech and a free press since the passage of the Bill of Rights in 1791. Though much of the concern was over political speech, morality was at issue as well. The U.S. Congress passed the Tariff Law of 1842, which limited the importation of obscene materials. And in 1873 a tougher antiobscenity law, the Comstock Law, was passed. It was named for Anthony Comstock, a founder of the New York Society for the Suppression of Vice, which fought against indecent art and behavior.

One common reason given for book banning throughout history has been the protection of the moral and ethical values of young people. The belief is that some works of art or literature can damage or destroy those values. Throughout history, children have not had the same rights as adults, and parents or other adults often had complete control over their children. Author Marjorie Heins writes in *Not in Front of the Children*: "The assumption was that … children and adolescents either are too fragile to handle vulgarity, sex, and controversy or lack the intellectual freedom rights that the First Amendment grants adults—or both."[4] Censorship and book banning grew out of the idea that children needed someone else to make decisions for them. The belief was that children could not make these decisions themselves. In the middle to late 1900s, censorship and book banning became a major issue in politics and public education.

Island Trees v. Pico is one of the most famous cases involving book banning in U.S. schools. This case took place in 1982 in the Island Trees Union Free School

District in New York. The board of education wanted some books removed from the school library, including *The Fixer, Laughing Boy, Black Boy, Go Ask Alice, Best Short Stories by Negro Writers, The Naked Ape, Down These Mean Streets, Soul on Ice, A Hero Ain't Nothin' but a Sandwich, A Reader for Writers,* and *Slaughterhouse-Five*.[5] They said the books were "anti-American, anti Christian, anti-Semitic, and just plain filthy."[6]

Student Steven Pico filed a lawsuit against the board, stating that the banning violated the students' First Amendment rights. The case made it to the Supreme Court, where the nine justices decided that Pico was right. The decision stated that the board could not ban the books based on their personal opinions and values and could not keep the books out of the library.[7]

Does this mean that book banning cannot or does

The Most Frequently Challenged Books of 1990–2000

1. Scary Stories (series) by Alvin Schwartz
2. *Daddy's Roommate* by Michael Willhoite
3. *I Know Why the Caged Bird Sings* by Maya Angelou
4. *The Chocolate War* by Robert Cormier
5. *Adventures of Huckleberry Finn* by Mark Twain
6. *Of Mice and Men* by John Steinbeck
7. Harry Potter (series) by J. K. Rowling
8. *Forever* by Judy Blume
9. *Bridge to Terabithia* by Katherine Paterson
10. Alice (series) by Phyllis Reynolds Naylor[8]

Teenagers in a school library. Throughout history, some have believed that young people need guidance about what they should read.

not happen in schools? No. *Island Trees* v. *Pico* determined that a school must go through a process when deciding whether to remove a book from the school library. If the book is removed because of a person's or a group's personal beliefs, that violates the First Amendment. However, if the book in question contains material considered "pervasively vulgar," the book can be removed.[9] The difficulty is determining what is vulgar, because people's opinions vary a great deal. The review process is supposed to help with this, ensuring that many people view the material as vulgar before a school library removes the book.

Book banning also occurs in the classroom. Some people object to certain books that are part of the curriculum, or study plan. Parents may ask that their child not read certain books based on religious or other personal opinions. In these instances, the student may read an alternate book. If the parent or another group tries to keep the book from all students, this is a form of censorship. Two of John Steinbeck's books are frequently included in high school curricula—*Of Mice and Men* and *The Grapes of Wrath*. Since their publication, both books have frequently been challenged or banned, though the former has been banned more often.

In the introduction to *Banned Books: Literature Suppressed on Political Grounds*, Ken Wachsberger writes that censorship has been widespread despite America's pride in the Bill of Rights, which in the First Amendment guarantees the rights to freedom of speech and religion:

17

Censorship has been a major part of American history from the time of Roger Williams and other early colonial freethinkers. Many of our richest literary works—*The Adventures of Huckleberry Finn, The Color Purple, The Grapes of Wrath, The Jungle, Uncle Tom's Cabin, Tropic of Cancer*—have been censored at one time or another. Even today school boards, local governments, religious fanatics and moral crusaders attempt to restrict our fredom to read.[10]

Who Bans Books?

Many people believe that only religious or politically conservative people ban books. Conservatives are often in the spotlight of book-challenging cases. Some argue that these people are responsible for most book-challenging cases. While these cases are the ones that seem to make the news, both conservative and liberal people want books banned, but for different reasons. Webster's dictionary defines *vulgar* as "offensive in language" and "lewdly or profanely indecent."[11] People interpret these definitions differently. Someone with religious or moral concerns might feel that any book with sexual content is vulgar. Someone else might feel that a book with racial terms is offensive in language. These types of arguments are used in book banning and come from people with differing beliefs, religious backgrounds, and political views.

18

In the introduction to his book *Banned in the U.S.A.* (2002), author Herbert N. Foerstel writes: "The older conservative organizations continue to seek out hints of vulgarity and mysticism in books for children and young adults, but liberal groups have also attempted to ban books containing violence and racial epithets. This emerging censorship combination bodes ill for free expression."[12]

Censorship occurs in subtle ways. Even material used in standardized tests is censored through an approval process. Someone has to approve reading passages used on tests. This process involves many people. For example, some types of publishers create materials purchased by state schools for testing. The publisher hires an author to write test passages and gives the author guidelines to follow. These guidelines include information about what types of

What Is Objectionable Speech?

What is objectionable speech?
Viewpoints about this can vary from one person to the next; however, there are some common reasons for challenging a book based on its language.

- **Swearing or cursing** includes impolite words that show anger and hatred and often involve divine punishment, such as *damn* or *hell*.
- **Profanity** involves using words that show contempt or disrespect for God, religious people or ideas, or things that are sacred.
- **Obscene language** often refers to things or ideas that many consider disgusting or repulsive, including vulgar sexual terms.
- **Racial or ethnic slurs** are words that intentionally mock, put down, or otherwise demean people of a particular race and/or ethnic group, such as *honky* or *spic*.
- **Defamation** is false speech that injures others; it includes libel and slander.

Other offensive language may demean people of a certain gender, age, sexual orientation, body type, or any other characteristic that someone wants to put down or debase.

subjects are permissible to write about and what words may or may not be used.

Author Diane Ravitch, a historian and professor at New York University, expresses concerns about the selection process for standardized tests in her book *The Language Police*. Ravitch worked in education for many years and also served as an assistant secretary in the U.S. Department of Education under George H.W. Bush. Ravitch worries that the idea of political correctness (writing and speaking in ways that will not offend anyone) is taken too far with standardized tests. She argues that the adults who choose books for the curricula and review and select test passages are so concerned about not offending anyone that the results have little to do with education and alter history.[13] For example, to avoid gender discrimination, titles or works that use words such as *man* or *men* instead of *humankind* or *people* are not allowed in some instances.

The idea of censoring materials used on standardized tests also affects passages from literature. In 2003, Jeanne Heifetz discovered that literary passages on New York Regents high school exams had been altered. Potentially offensive words and ideas were removed. Why is this a problem? Heifetz argued that, by removing these words, the testers had changed the meaning of the texts. She argued that students would not fully understand the author's meaning. Ravitch writes, "She found that the majority of passages had been altered to remove references to race, religion, alcohol, profanity, and sex as well as other purportedly controversial

20

subjects."[14] Although Heifetz's actions brought attention to the problem, altered passages were still included in tests afterward.[15]

While censoring test passages may seem harmless, limiting learning materials extends beyond tests. Almost all learning materials used in schools are censored to some degree. By applying rules similar to those for standardized tests, for example, Steinbeck's book *Of Mice and Men* is inappropriate because it has "men" in the title. For some people, the title is not the issue, of course; they do not like the subject matter and language used in the book. But Ravitch uses this title as one of many examples.[16] She argues that too much concern over offending readers leads to a dull and inaccurate education.

Is book banning and censorship a bad thing? Many people who wish to have books removed from the schools

Terms Related to Book Censorship

ban—To remove a book or other material from a library or school curriculum.

censor—To prevent the publication or dissemination of material that is considered objectionable, sensitive, or harmful.

challenge—To file a formal protest against the inclusion of a book in a library.

restict—To limit the circulation of a book to people of a particular age or those who have parental approval.

believe that it will benefit the students. Whether a book is removed because of offensive language or because it deals with difficult themes such as sexuality, the reason given is often to protect students or to provide some benefit. Oftentimes, people who wish to ban books are not trying to be mean or to limit a person's rights. Instead, they wish to promote what they see as positive values by limiting books with negative or controversial themes. For example, restricting books that use racial slurs might help avoid situations that hurt students' self-esteem. In other words, people who wish to remove books from the schools usually believe that they are acting in a positive way for the students.

Gateways to Education is an organization dedicated to keeping the Christian faith in the public school system. In an article on challenging books in the schools, writer Eric Buehrer discusses the difficulty in defining what censorship is. He writes: "Educators shouldn't describe what a parent wants to do in seeking to remove a book as censorship and describe what schools do every day as selection." What he is saying is that when parents want certain books removed from the schools, it is called censorship. Yet, someone has to decide in the first place what books will or will not be part of the curriculum. This process is called "selection" in the public school system.

Buehrer argues that both decisions involve the same process. He writes: "When a parent questions the validity of a book in school, we call it a censorship challenge. But when the teacher does it, we call it part of the job. Maybe censorship is part of the job!" Buehrer concludes: "The only suitable definition of a censor is the one found in the dictionary: 'one authorized to examine material, as literature or plays, and remove or suppress anything considered objectionable.'"[17]

Using the Supreme Court's ruling in *Island Trees* v. *Pico* as a guide, Buehrer provides a checklist for those who wish to challenge a book in a school. One of the primary issues is the school's policy on "profanity," and whether or not the book violates that policy. Gateways to Education's Web site provides additional information on how to go about challenging a book, again using the guidelines set forth by *Island Trees* v. *Pico*. It stresses that challenges must follow certain guidelines. As determined in the Supreme Court ruling, a book must be "pervasively vulgar" or "educationally unsuitable"[18] to a number of people to qualify for removal.

Is censorship necessary? Do children need protecting? The bottom line is that not everyone agrees about what is best for students. The terms *pervasively vulgar* and *educationally unsuitable* mean different things to different people. Author Marjorie Heins writes: "Even if adults could agree, moreover, on what is truly inadvisable for young people, the rarely asked question remains, In what sense is it harmful? And does it justify censorship?"[19] The question about whether certain materials do in fact cause harm is difficult to answer. Individuals are affected differently by all kinds of input, including music, television, games, and books.

23

There will always be someone who finds some materials offensive, whether it is because of content, racial language, or gender stereotyping (among many other issues). Ultimately, it is up to each individual to decide what is best for him or her. However, in school, students' access to some information is limited to some degree, depending on who designs the curriculum and how the school defines offensiveness.

In addition to the issues already discussed, political censorship has also enjoyed a long history. Governments have often restricted what information people may access. Under some governments, authorities decide what people may talk about, watch on television or in films, or read. Even in the United States, where freedom of speech and religion are constitutional rights under the First Amendment, political censorship has occurred. How does this affect what students read? Governments run public schools. City and state governments have the most direct influence on schools.

U.S. citizens, including students, have the right to read and speak about different topics to the extent allowed by the law. However, until children are of a certain age (eighteen in most states), parents have the right to determine what their children have access to. This can include what their children read in school. This does not necessarily mean that they can make the decision about what other people's children are allowed to read. However, in all situations, some person or group decides which books will be a part of the curricula and what books will be in the school library.

Chapter 3

Steinbeck: A Life in Search of Truth

John Steinbeck wrote about many topics, and he did not shy away from controversial ones. While he did not seek out controversy, he was determined to write about issues important to him. In some of his most relevant work, he sought to draw attention to social issues that affected many people in the United States. Steinbeck had a great interest in the common worker and common experiences. This entered his work in many ways. Of his numerous books, two or three most often find their ways onto banned books lists. These books deal with social issues in America as well as controversial topics such as religion and sexuality. Steinbeck wrote from his own perspective on life. How did that perspective develop?

On February 27, 1902, in a home in Salinas, California, Olive Hamilton Steinbeck gave birth to

John Steinbeck, shown here in a 1966 photo, wrote about issues he believed were central to the American experience.

a son, John Ernst Steinbeck, named after his father (although the older Steinbeck was known as Ernst). John was the third of four children and the only boy. Steinbeck's parents had met in California, but both were descendants of European immigrants. As a boy, Steinbeck heard his grandparents' stories, and many themes from those stories entered his fiction later in life. One primary theme in many of Steinbeck's books is the idea of leaving a familiar place to seek out something better. This is what the immigrants did when they came to America. They hoped to find a better life and make their fortune. This is also a running theme throughout much of Western literature, which Steinbeck enjoyed reading.

Steinbeck's father worked at a few jobs before becoming treasurer for Montgomery County in California. He stayed in this job for many years, until his death in 1935. Although he spent his working life in an office, the elder Steinbeck's passion lay in the outdoors. He enjoyed working in the garden and riding his horse. While his father was reserved, Steinbeck's mother, Olive, was more outgoing. She obtained her teaching certificate at age seventeen, something uncommon for a woman at that time. Prior to meeting Ernst, she taught in many one-room schoolhouses. When she married, she shifted her focus to community organizations to help improve the town of Salinas. Olive Steinbeck helped instill a love of reading and words in her son by giving him books. One of his favorite stories was that of King Arthur. Later, as an adult, Steinbeck had plans to write a version of the King Arthur story. (He worked on it periodically, and an unfinished version was published after his death.) The influences and experiences of Steinbeck's parents and grandparents later showed up in many of his works, as did the Salinas area. As a youth, John also enjoyed spending time outdoors, taking in his surroundings.

As the only boy in the family, John was treated differently from his sisters, Elizabeth, Esther, and Mary. His parents spoiled him a bit, but perhaps they expected more from him as well. He had rules to follow, but he also had a mischievous streak. For example, he took up smoking at an early age, taking pains to hide it from his parents. When his father discovered John's habit, rather than quit, John simply hid it better.[1] This type of thinking and ability to outwit others helped Steinbeck write such works as the *The Moon is Down*, which dealt with espionage during World War II. Years later, when asked how he "knew" wartime secrets, he replied, "I guessed. I just put myself in your place and thought what I would do."[2]

Steinbeck's school years alternated between periods of withdrawal and socialization. He often spent time outdoors alone. Some early childhood friends described John as a loner, while others remembered him as more of a leader, getting himself and his friends into trouble. He did not have many friends in his teen years, however. His younger sister, Mary, was one of his few friends during that time.[3] They frequently acted out scenes from the King Arthur stories. This pattern of periods of social interaction alternating with periods of withdrawal continued throughout Steinbeck's life.

Steinbeck's parents expected him to earn his own spending money. He took a job delivering papers, but he did not do well. He often delivered the papers late or not at all. He also took jobs helping farmers, a common business in California. In these jobs, Steinbeck met and worked alongside homeless migrant workers. These men traveled from one job to another, never staying in one place for long. They often traveled with the seasons, as available work changed during different times of the year. These homeless workers were called bindle stiffs because of the sacks, or bindles, that they carried over their shoulders. They later showed up as characters in Steinbeck's fiction.

Becoming a Writer

In 1919, Steinbeck entered Stanford University in Palo Alto, California, as an English major. He did not take the required courses, but he focused instead on those courses that he thought would help him in his writing career. Steinbeck had known since his early teens that he wanted to write. At the university, he felt some courses were not worth his time. He repeated other courses, however, feeling that they helped his writing and were enjoyable. During his time in college, he met a good friend, Carlton Sheffield, who went by the name "Duke," or "Dook," as Steinbeck spelled it. The two became lifelong friends.

In order to pay for his schooling, Steinbeck alternated between taking a semester or two at college and working to save money for more classes. Many of his jobs involved physical labor. These experiences also shaped his later writing. He saw many people working hard but barely making enough money to live on. Steinbeck felt that other people needed to know about workers who endured harsh working conditions and inequality. Working themes and the plights of laborers found their way into many of Steinbeck's works.

After six years of attending college on and off, Steinbeck left Stanford to travel to New York City, where he felt he could be more successful in starting a writing career. This decision led to some difficult times.

Steinbeck arrived in New York with very little money. He traveled there by boat, taking a long journey around much of South America. Steinbeck's older sister, Beth, lived in Brooklyn with her husband, who helped Steinbeck find a construction job building Madison Square Garden. The work was difficult with long hours. Upon coming home, Steinbeck felt too tired to write. Later, Steinbeck's uncle helped him obtain a position as a reporter with the *New York American*. This, too, became a difficult job. Steinbeck had trouble finishing stories or getting them to his editor on time. After a few months on the job, the paper fired him. With little money and several failed attempts at getting his fiction published, Steinbeck returned to California.

In 1926, Steinbeck took a job as a family and house caretaker at Lake Tahoe, a popular vacation spot on the border between California and Nevada. He took care of the family when they were there, and he helped teach the children. When the family left during the winter, Steinbeck took care of the house and wrote. While there, he completed his first published novel, *Cup of Gold*. This story was inspired in part by his boat trip to New York. He also wrote *To a God Unknown*.

In 1928, Steinbeck met Carol Henning in Tahoe City, where she was vacationing. Steinbeck moved to San Francisco in 1928 to be closer to Carol. There, he took a warehouse job, again doing long hours of physically exhausting work. He continued to write and to see Carol. He received financial help from a friend so he could keep writing. In addition, Steinbeck's father offered him a place to stay in a family home in Pacific Grove, California. There, Steinbeck could live rent free, and his father provided him with twenty-five dollars a month. It was enough to help Steinbeck meet his living expenses and continue to write full-time. He had goals he wanted to reach. One was to become a published author. He knew he needed to polish his writing skills, which he did during this time. He also wanted to marry Carol, but he wanted to wait until he could support himself.

In 1929, Steinbeck heard from Robert M. McBride and Company, a New York publisher that had previously rejected his work. They were interested in his first novel, *Cup of Gold*. It was published later that same year. Steinbeck and Carol married in January of 1930. They lived in Eagle Rock, California, near Dook Sheffield. Money was tight, and the couple moved often. Even though Steinbeck was a published author now, he still received money from his father. This was early in the Great Depression, which began when the stock market crashed in October of 1929. The couple decided to move back to the Steinbeck home in Pacific Grove, California. There, they could grow food in the garden and fish the sea. This living arrangement, while still difficult for the couple, allowed Steinbeck to continue writing.

Steinbeck met another friend who would become a prominent influence on his philosophy and writing. Ed Ricketts was a biologist who worked along Cannery Row, an area where sardines were processed. People of various ethnic backgrounds worked in the canneries. When visiting Ricketts, Steinbeck observed and got to know many of those workers. Once again, the experiences of these workers made an impression upon him and would later enter his fictionalized accounts of working life in America.

Ricketts was a biologist who developed specimens for high school and college biology students. He also had specific views about nature, and he felt that humans placed too much emotion on natural occurrences. He believed that there was no "good" or "evil" in nature. Instead, animals, including people, simply act for survival. Placing moral values on these acts can be defined as *teleological* thinking. An example of this is thinking that a lion's killing a zebra is cruel. From Steinbeck's and Ricketts's non-teleological point of view, this kind of action by the lion is simply a means of survival. Steinbeck described non-teleological thinking in a book he wrote with Ricketts called *Sea of Cortez*. He wrote: "Non-teleological thinking concerns itself primarily not with what should be, or could be, or might be, but rather with what actually 'is'—attempting at most to answer the already sufficiently difficult questions *what* or *how*, instead *of why*."[4] In other words, rather than looking at the cause and effects of things (why), non-teleological thinking looks simply at what is (what and how). Concepts involving this type of thinking also made their way into Steinbeck's fiction, including *The Grapes of Wrath*.

Steinbeck also applied these ideas to a book of stories, *The Pastures of Heaven*. When he was ready to publish this collection late in 1931, he contacted a new literary agency in New York. The agency, McIntosh and Otis, was founded by Mavis McIntosh and Elizabeth Otis. The two women and Steinbeck were to become longtime friends, and the literary agency became well known and highly respected. The women sold the *Pastures of Heaven* manuscript in 1932. Later that same year, Steinbeck's mother, Olive, suffered a stroke and later died. While his mother was ill, Steinbeck and Carol moved to Salinas to take care of her. This difficult time affected Steinbeck, as family was important to him.

The Cannery Row neighborhood in Monterey, California. This historic district was featured in several of Steinbeck's books.

While caring for his mother, Steinbeck developed another theory about life. He saw humans as individual cells of a larger group, or body. He called the larger body the phalanx. Some events that affected the phalanx, such as wars and the Great Depression, were much bigger than any one individual. He argued that the larger body had a will of its own. In other words, a group becomes a new entity, where the "strength of such a group exceeds the sum of its parts."[5] For example, people in a group often think and act in ways that are best for the group but not necessarily best for each individual. These ideas of the phalanx made their way into Steinbeck's fiction, such as *The Grapes of Wrath*. This story shows the Great Depression from an individual point of view and as a larger issue created by and affecting the phalanx.

Steinbeck continued writing while caring for his mother. He completed many works, including The *Long Valley*, *The Red Pony*, and *Tortilla Flat*. He faced difficulty publishing them, however, as the Depression affected many publishers, including the ones who had published his previous works. However, toward the end of 1934, things started to turn around.

Back in New York, editor Pascal Covici overheard a bookseller recommending the works of John Steinbeck to a customer. Covici purchased the books, and he liked what he read. He tracked down Steinbeck through McIntosh and Otis. The publishing company, Covici-Friede, offered to publish *Tortilla Flat* and to reprint both of Steinbeck's previously published books. Bad news came along with the good: Steinbeck's father had fallen ill. Worn down and exhausted from caring for his wife, Olive, in her illness, and depressed over her death, Steinbeck's father passed away in 1935.

After a long struggle to be published and his parents' illnesses and deaths, Steinbeck and Carol decided to get away. They took a three-month trip to Mexico, using money from the sale of *Tortilla Flat*. While there, they enjoyed the vacation, but Steinbeck did not write as he had planned to do. They returned home to learn that while they were away, *Tortilla Flat* had become a best seller. Steinbeck did not like the idea of fame. He worried that it would affect his ongoing work. He also wanted his writing to stand on its own. He did not want his personality to affect the way readers perceived his work. When he gave interviews, he only answered questions about the work and did not reveal much personal information. This approach led to various theories about who he was, but this did not bother him much. His primary concern was the work itself, not what other people thought of him.

Labor Themes

Although *Tortilla Flat* was a book with a lot of humor, his next work, *In Dubious Battle*, focused on a common theme throughout many of his books: the plight of the common worker. This book focused on the strikes of California's farmworkers, many of whom came from varied ethnic backgrounds. They were marginalized, or viewed as separate from—and less than—the average American. The strikes in California were often violent. The power of the large farming community and large numbers of people looking for work resulted in very low wages during and after the Depression. To learn more, Steinbeck interviewed many workers. He often paid them for their stories.

36

The fictional account in the book *In Dubious Battle* not only related stories based on real workers, but also included Steinbeck's philosophies. He applied both his non-teleological views and his thoughts on the phalanx. Steinbeck also experimented with the form of this book. Experimenting was something Steinbeck would do in many of his works. In this book, he left out the conclusion, because the strikes were still going on when the book came out. He didn't know how the real stories would end. When the book was published in 1936, it did well, with few objections. Those who did not like the book argued that Steinbeck supported Communist ideas.

To avoid some of the pitfalls of fame, John and Carol Steinbeck moved to a more reclusive area near Los Gatos, California. They bought a small house, and Steinbeck began work on a story that he incorrectly thought would have limited appeal. The book started out with the title *Something That Happened*. When published in 1937, the title had been changed to *Of Mice and Men*. Once again, Steinbeck experimented with form. This time, he wrote the story like a play that focused on two migrant workers. Steinbeck wanted to portray the characters as accurately as possible so his characters spoke language considered profane by many people. *Of Mice and Men* also included sexual references. This type of character portrayal influenced the book's history of becoming one of the most-often banned or challenged books throughout the twentieth century and into the twenty-first.

Meanwhile, an editor with the *San Francisco News* asked Steinbeck to write some articles about migrant workers in California. He agreed. To research his articles, Steinbeck once again went straight to the source. The Great Depression had created a large migration of people from the Midwest and Southwest. A combination of drought and banking practices left many farmers out of work. Thousands of people migrated across the country after hearing that California farmers needed workers. These people found little work and very poor living conditions. They lived in tents in small, disorganized communities, often without running water. Steinbeck witnessed their struggles firsthand, even living with them for a time in order to gain a full understanding of the situation. Steinbeck's original assignment for the newspaper led to his writing a book, which he started in 1938. *The Grapes of Wrath* was published in 1939.

Challenges

The book tackled many issues, not just those of the migrant workers. Steinbeck once again depicted characters based on his interviews, using language of the time. He included his non-teleological views and questioned organized religion through his characters. He wrote about prejudices, questioned authority figures, and addressed political issues that affected the lives of many people. The book was a huge commercial success, and it brought attention to a situation that many Americans did not know about. However, some people protested and banned or challenged the book immediately. This included some farmers' associations, political figures, and others who simply did not like the language and issues in the novel. *The Grapes of Wrath*, too, became a frequently challenged book.

In 1939, Kern County, California, launched a campaign to remove the book from all its libraries, stating that the book portrayed its citizens in a bad light. The movement was organized in part by the Associated Farmers. One of Steinbeck's biographers, Jackson J. Benson, writes about Steinbeck's reaction:

> Steinbeck had a genuine fear of retribution by the Associated Farmers for his pro-farm labor writings. He had seen what he believed to be evidence of intimidation by violence, blackmail, and extortion on the part of the Associated Farmers and other grower organizations and believed that they were capable of anything.[6]

Steinbeck's fame grew with the success of *The Grapes of Wrath*. However, the process of writing and publishing the book had drained him, physically and emotionally. At this point, he decided to focus on nonfiction. He and Ed Ricketts wrote about science. Along with Carol, they set out on a boat trip in 1940, sailing south along the West Coast. The journey inspired *Sea of Cortez* and other works, such as *The Pearl*. Upon their return, Steinbeck wrote a screenplay, *The Forgotten Village*, about the use of modern medicine

Marine biologist Edward Ricketts, Steinbeck's good friend, was the inspiration for the character of Doc in the books *Cannery Row* and *Sweet Thursday*.

in a small Mexican town. This was a time of great conflict and upheaval in the world, as the Second World War had started. It was also a time of personal conflict for Steinbeck, who faced an ongoing strep infection and marital problems with Carol. The couple separated, and Steinbeck moved to New York.

In 1941, Steinbeck attended a conference in Washington, D.C., about propaganda. Steinbeck had previously been in contact with President Franklin D. Roosevelt about this subject. Propaganda is information deliberately spread to influence the ideas of others; often it is not completely true or balanced. The president had concerns about Nazi propaganda spreading throughout Mexico. Roosevelt asked Steinbeck to help create antipropaganda materials. Steinbeck agreed. His involvement in politics and the government affected his fiction, just as his other experiences had. His novel *The Moon is Down*, published in 1942, portrayed a European country under a Nazi-like influence. The novel inspired some political concern. World War II was not yet over, and some people worried that the book might prove to be more fact than fiction.

John and Carol Steinbeck divorced in 1943. Shortly afterward, Steinbeck married Gwyndolyn Conger, known as Gwyn, whom he had met through a friend. Soon after, Steinbeck traveled to Europe and Africa to report on the war for a newspaper, the *New York Herald Tribune*. As he had earlier, Steinbeck focused on stories of individuals rather than reporting on the overall war efforts. After returning home in the fall of 1943, Steinbeck opted to write a lighter piece of fiction. He felt that what he learned of the war was too emotional for fiction. Instead, he wrote *Cannery Row*, published in 1945. The inspiration for the book came from his work with Ed Ricketts and the people he had met on Cannery Row in California. Between writing the book and its publication date, John and Gwyn Steinbeck had a baby boy, Thom, born on August 2, 1944. The couple worked on the film version of *The Pearl* throughout 1945. They welcomed their second child, John Steinbeck IV, on June 12, 1946. Steinbeck completed work on *The Wayward Bus* the following October.

The Steinbecks traveled for a while. Their travels included a trip to Scandinavia where Steinbeck received the Liberty Cross from the king of Norway for *The Moon is Down*.[7] It was the first time a non-Norwegian received the medal.[8] The couple experienced growing troubles. Steinbeck was often away, including an extensive trip in 1948 to California to research an upcoming novel. Shortly after his return, Steinbeck received word that his good friend Ed Ricketts had suffered serious injuries after a car accident. Steinbeck returned to California, but Ricketts passed away before Steinbeck arrived. The loss was hard for Steinbeck, and when he returned home, Gwyn announced that she wanted a divorce.

Steinbeck became depressed and remained so for some months, but continued some screenplay work. He eventually settled back into a regular writing schedule. He also fell in love again. He married Elaine Anderson

Scott in late 1950, and a period of productivity followed. He worked on stage and screen material and a book in memory of Ed Ricketts, entitled *The Log From the Sea of Cortez*. He also continued working on the book he had researched in California. It was published as *East of Eden* in 1952.

East of Eden was a large work. Steinbeck had learned from writing *The Grapes of Wrath* that a large undertaking was very tiring. For *East of Eden*, Steinbeck limited himself to writing only eight hundred to one thousand words per day. His wife, Elaine, supported Steinbeck's work by allowing him the quiet time he needed when he was working and providing opportunities for him to rest and relax. The novel interwove his family's history with a fictional story. Steinbeck viewed the novel as his masterpiece. It combined his personal history, fiction, and biblical story lines. He also viewed the novel as a gift to his sons. The themes throughout the book include family relationships, especially those between brothers. It parallels the biblical story of Cain and Abel.

After Steinbeck finished the novel in 1952, he and Elaine traveled to Europe. Travel continued to be a regular interest for the couple. They kept their home in New York City so Steinbeck could be close to his sons, whom he saw regularly. In the early 1950s, Steinbeck worked on a variety of creative projects, including *East of Eden*, journalism pieces, and other shorter works. He was also involved in politics. Steinbeck showed public support of other creative figures, such as playwright

Arthur Miller, during the mid-1950s when a fear of communism spread throughout the country.

To escape city life, the Steinbecks purchased a cottage in Sag Harbor on Long Island. There, Steinbeck found peace and quiet that allowed him to work. He began working on a project he had wanted to write for many years: a retelling of King Arthur's tales. After struggling with the stories, he and Elaine traveled to England at her suggestion. She thought he might find inspiration at the actual locations where the stories took place. However, even after Steinbeck started writing again, he was not pleased with his work. He wanted the stories to be perfect.

He also began publicly commenting on American life during this time. He was not happy with what he saw as the growing materialism in the country. A letter he had written stating that the country's wealth would cause its downfall aroused controversy. By this time, Steinbeck was familiar with creating this kind of reaction. Some of his most popular books caused some type of controversy. Rather than shy away from the reaction, Steinbeck did what he did best. He wrote a book about how he viewed the country's wealth and its affect on people. The book would be his last novel. *The Winter of Our Discontent* was published in 1961.

Upon completion of the novel, Steinbeck wanted to get back in touch with everyday people. Although he had experienced some health issues, he set out on a road trip across the country with his dog Charlie. They traveled through many states and visited Salinas, which had changed considerably since Steinbeck's youth. He chronicled the trip in *Travels With Charley: In Search of America*, published in 1962. That year would be one to remember.

Recognition

In late October 1962, Steinbeck learned that he had won the Nobel Prize for Literature. While this award is often presented for a single novel, in this case, the award was for Steinbeck's body of work. The nomination came with both praise and criticism. Some people felt that he had not written anything worthwhile for nearly twenty years. Even Steinbeck himself commented that he did not believe he deserved the award. Despite this statement, Steinbeck was upset when many literary critics publicly agreed with him. He did not write fiction again. The prize created a renewed interest in his stories, however, and book sales increased dramatically. Steinbeck, who had avoided public speaking as much as possible throughout his career, delivered an acceptance speech at the award ceremony, which authors Jeffrey Schultz and Luchen Li refer to as one "of remarkable grace."[9] Early in the speech, he acknowledged both his feelings of doubt as well as excitement when he said, "In my heart there may be doubt that I deserve the Nobel award over other men of letters whom I hold in respect and reverence—but there is no question of my pleasure and pride in having it for myself."[10] He also said, "The writer is delegated to declare and to celebrate man's proven capacity for greatness of heart and spirit—for gallantry in defeat—for courage, compassion and love. In the endless war against weakness and despair, these are the bright rally-flags of hope and of emulation."[11]

Steinbeck toured behind the Iron Curtain at the request of President Kennedy in 1963, receiving mixed receptions from his audiences in the Soviet Union, Poland, Hungary, Czechoslovakia, and West Berlin.[12] Steinbeck met privately with people so that he could hear their views. Following his return home, President Lyndon Johnson gave Steinbeck the Medal of Freedom in September of 1964. The two men became friends. Elaine Steinbeck and Johnson's wife, Lady Bird, had attended college together. Their renewed friendship helped form one between Steinbeck and the president.

The Steinbecks traveled to Vietnam in 1966 in an effort to understand the war. John Steinbeck went as a reporter for *Newsday* to write about the war. He had been of the opinion that Americans should support the efforts of the military. After viewing the war firsthand, he ultimately questioned the role of the United States in the conflict. However, he supported the soldiers. Both of his sons had joined the military in 1966.

Steinbeck experienced recurring health scares in the early 1960s that continued throughout the remainder of his life. Following surgery to relieve pain in his back in October 1967, Steinbeck felt well enough to travel to the Virgin Islands with Elaine in December. He wanted to do more traveling, but he knew his health was failing. Ongoing heart problems had grown worse in the summer of 1968. On December 20, 1968, he died peacefully in his New York apartment with his wife, Elaine, at his side. At his service, she said, "All I ask is—remember him. Remember him!"[13] Her request was granted. Steinbeck's work continues to be read and recognized for its quality, experimental techniques, reflection of humanity, and storytelling.

Many recurring themes throughout Steinbeck's life affected the literature that led to the Nobel Prize. His family's history, the people he grew up with, and the Salinas Valley made their way into his books in various forms. His societal views, non-teleological thinking, and his phalanx theory intertwined with religion and biblical themes. Place and setting also play important, recurrent roles in Steinbeck's novels. Additionally, Steinbeck's ongoing desire to understand the individual allowed him to get to know all sorts of people, including many not readily accepted by society. His portrayal of migrant workers and bindle stiffs led to some of his greatest literary works. His travels, both abroad and throughout the country, are mirrored in his characters' needs to migrate, find a better life, and ultimately understand themselves and their situations more fully.

Chapter 4

Of Mice and Men

Of Mice and Men is a novella, or short novel, published in 1937, two years before *The Grapes of Wrath*. It is Steinbeck's sixth novel. Since its publication, it has often been included in high school curricula, and it has frequently been challenged or banned. As with much of Steinbeck's writing, he experimented with the form. The novel's format is similar to that of a play. It uses a lot of dialogue, is short, and focuses on character and action. Because it is shorter than a conventional novel, the story does not have traditional chapters; it is broken instead into various scenes. Steinbeck used this format because he wanted to reach people who did not read longer works. Steinbeck adapted it for the stage, and it has been adapted as an opera and into several film versions by others.

The title of the work also changed from the original, *Something That Happened*. Either Steinbeck's first wife, Carol, or his friend Ed Ricketts, read Steinbeck a poem, "To a Mouse," by Robert Burns. The poem contains the lines, "The best laid schemes o' mice and men/Gang aft a-gley." (The phrase "gang aft a-gley" is usually translated from the Scots dialect as "oft go astray.") Steinbeck liked the line, which relates to a major theme of the story: people and situations going awry. He used part of it as the new title for his work.[1]

The story focuses on two main characters, George Milton and Lennie Small, bindle stiffs who moved from place to place as their work took them. George plays a protective and fatherly role to Lennie, who is big, strong, and mentally disabled. Lennie unwittingly makes many mistakes along their travels, and George frequently has to make excuses for his friend. Lennie is often not aware of his own strength. He likes to pet small, soft animals, but he has a history of accidentally killing them. Lennie's most recent troubles occurred when he wanted to feel the material of a girl's dress, and she thought he was trying to hurt her. George obviously cares about Lennie and knows that without him, Lennie would end up in some type of trouble. They keep each other company along their travels from one job to another.

Plot Summary

As the story opens, George and Lennie are on the road, camping beside a river. George reminds Lennie that they are starting a new job because Lennie got into trouble after trying to touch a girl's dress. George discovers that Lennie has a dead mouse in his pocket so he can pet it. Disgusted, George throws the mouse into the

During the Depression, men like George and Lennie traveled from job to job, carrying their belongings in sacks, or bindles. This man was photographed in California in 1938.

woods, but Lennie finds it and hides it again. They talk about how lucky they are to have each other for company and about how they will buy their own land some day and "live off the fatta the lan'." George tells Lennie that he will have rabbits to pet and take care of. George also tells Lennie that if he gets into any kind of trouble at the new job, he should come back to the river and hide.

When the men arrive at the new job, they meet the other workers: Candy, an old man; Crooks, the black stable hand; Slim; and Carlson. They also meet the boss; his son, Curley, a former boxer; and Curley's pretty young wife. Candy has an old, stinky dog that the other men want to get rid of. Carlson offers to take the dog out and shoot it. Knowing that the dog is old and in pain, Candy agrees. He climbs onto his bunk, and the men can see that he is crying. Slim's dog recently had puppies, and Carlson suggests that Slim give one of them to Candy. He does, and gives one of the puppies to Lennie as well.

Curley comes in looking for his wife. He notices that Slim is not there. The men guess that Curley suspects Slim is with his wife. When Lennie returns, George warns him not to get involved in any fights. George and Lennie start talking about the place they want to own someday. Candy listens, and the men agree that Candy can be a part of the plan. Slim returns with Curley, and they argue. Curley does not want to fight with Slim, so he attacks Lennie instead. Not wanting to fight back, Lennie begs George to make Curley stop.

George tells Lennie it is okay to defend himself. Lennie grabs one of Curley's hands and crushes it. Carlson takes Curley to the doctor. George tells Lennie that he did not do anything wrong. Lennie goes to the barn and the puppies, and Crooks invites him in to talk; Candy shows up later. They talk about the rabbits they will have on their farm. Crooks says he will work for them if they will let him. As he says this, Curley's wife walks in and asks if any of them have seen Curley. As they talk, she is rude to all of them. Crooks asks her to leave. She threatens him, implying that she could get him in a lot of trouble. The men back down, realizing that she has that power because she is white and married to Curley.

The next scene shows Lennie in the barn, crying because he has accidentally killed his puppy. Curley's wife walks in. Lennie tells her about the puppy. She consoles him saying that he can get another puppy. She moves closer to him. Curley's wife tells Lennie that her hair is soft. Lennie strokes it, and she becomes upset that he is messing it up. She gets angry and turns her head, but Lennie shakes her and accidentally kills her. Knowing he is in big trouble, Lennie runs away to the river. When Curley and the others find out, they decide to find Lennie and shoot him. Carlson's gun is missing, and they assume that Lennie took it. George asks Slim if they could bring Lennie back and lock him up instead. Slim tells George that would be worse for Lennie, and George hesitantly agrees. Curley insists that

George go with them to prove that he did not have anything to do with the murder.

George finds Lennie. To prevent him from being lynched by Curley and the other men, George shoots Lennie in the back of the head. George tells the others that he took Carlson's gun from Lennie and shot him. Slim understands that George's story is not true. George and Slim leave to go have a drink together.

Characters

While most of the characters in the story are bindle stiffs, each has a distinct personality. Steinbeck shows this through the characters' words, attitudes, and actions. One of the primary reasons the book is challenged is because of the characters' language.

Steinbeck's characters are realistic examples of how people in those situations really spoke, and this is offensive to some people. His characters use racial slurs, profanity, and swear words. Some people do not like reading these types of words. The words vary a great deal as well, and as a result, are potentially offensive to different types of people. For example, some people might be okay with swear words but not profanity, which uses religious names as swear words. Another person might not have a problem with profanity, but might be very offended by the racial slurs used in the book. In other words, the language used in the story has the potential to offend many people.

Objections to *Of Mice and Men* involve more than bad language, however. Steinbeck's focus on people who are marginalized, or shunned by society, also troubles some readers. The words and subject matter have offended some people both then and now, which is one reason why *Of Mice and Men* has been challenged frequently since its publication. The following is an overview of the main characters in the story.

Lennie Small. Lennie, a mentally disabled man, represents innocence and childlike behavior. He does not mean to cause harm, but he cannot help himself. Therefore, he is unable to function in society without someone watching out for him. Even then, George cannot keep Lennie out of trouble alltogether. Lennie's actions eventually get him into trouble that they cannot run away from.

Lennie is in many ways a stereotypical representation of a mentally challenged person. He is childlike, bumbles through life, remembers only certain things, and cannot control his physical strength. Lennie is offensive to some readers because he is a stereotypical character, and he does not represent mentally challenged people in a positive light. Just as some readers may not want to be exposed to racial or gender stereotypes, others do not want to be exposed to this type of stereotype, either.

George Milton. George acts much like a parent to Lennie. He watches out for Lennie as best he can. In contrast to Lennie, who is described as having a shapeless face, George has very strong, sharp features. He allows Lennie to dream that they can one day own their own farm. George understands that the dream will probably never happen. As a traveling worker, he seems to enjoy Lennie's innocent company. Most workers in their situation travel alone. The fact that George and Lennie travel together and share such a strong bond is unusual for men in their situation. Some of the other characters seem to question if their relationship is a homosexual one. Slim comments to George that it is "Funny how you an' him string along together."[2] In this conversation, Slim remarks that most people in their line of work travel alone and that it is odd that George and Lennie do not. The word "funny" implies homosexuality, not humor.

Slim. Slim is the mule driver on the farm. He is described as godlike, and he seems to know more than the rest of the men. At the end of the story, Slim understands what really happened between Lennie and George. Wanting to reassure George that he had no choice but to do what he did, Slim says, "You hadda, George. I swear you hadda."[3] Slim and George leave together to go have a drink, showing a bond and an understanding between the men. This action also provides a bit of hope at the end of the story, as the reader feels that George will be okay.

Curley. Curley is the boss's son. He is jealous of anyone who talks to his wife and spends much of his time tracking her down. The men tease him for keeping one of his hands "soft for his wife" inside a glove with Vaseline. As a boxer, he thinks he is tough, and he likes to pick on others. When he picks a fight with Lennie, he ends up with a crushed hand. He is the one who wants to go after Lennie at the end of the story and insists that George go along.

Curley's Wife. The men do not view Curley's wife in positive ways, but Steinbeck does not necessarily intend that the reader dislike her. She is a sympathetic character in several ways. First, she is the only female there and seemingly lonely. Her husband, Curley, is jealous and controlling, and she gave up her own dreams of becoming a movie star when she married. The men think she is a floozy because of the way she looks and acts, although it is possible that they are misinterpreting her actions. She may in fact simply be looking for someone to talk to. One example of this is when she interrupts Candy, Lennie, and Crooks talking in the barn. Candy accuses her of looking for trouble. Her response gives some insight into her marriage:

> He said accusingly, "You gotta husban'. You got no call foolin' aroun' with other guys, causin' trouble."

> The girl flared up. "Sure I gotta husban'. You all seen him. Swell guy, ain't he? Spends all his time sayin' what he's gonna do to guys he don't like, and he don' like nobody."[4]

Later in the conversation, when Candy and Crooks tell her to leave Lennie alone, she threatens Crooks. While she is not responsible for her death, her vanity creates the situation. She brags of her soft hair, not knowing Lennie's strength. Her death causes Curley and the other men to go after Lennie.

While Steinbeck's intention was to make her a sympathetic character, some readers still find her objectionable. In some ways, she is a stereotypical, one-dimensional character. She is also controlled by her husband, and she is shown as inferior to almost all the men in the story, not just Curley.

Candy. Candy is the old man who cleans the bunkhouse. He is the first man George and Lennie meet when they arrive. Candy has some money saved and wants to help buy a farm with Lennie and George. He has an old, feeble dog, which one of the other men shoots early in the novel. Later, he says that he should have been the one to shoot the dog because the dog was his responsibility. When talking to George, Candy says, "I ought to of shot that dog myself, George. I shouldn't ought to of let no stranger shoot my dog."[5] This line foreshadows the end of the story. George does not let strangers shoot Lennie.

Crooks. Crooks is the African-American stable hand. He is bent over because a horse once kicked him. He lives in the stable because he is black and the other men do not want to be around him. The men treat him as though he is worthless because of his age, race, and disability; however, in the description of his living quarters and in his dialogue, the reader sees that he is intelligent and lonely.

Themes

Even though the novel is short, a number of themes run through the story. Depending on how a reader interprets the story, any one of those themes may seem prominent. Some of the themes in the novel are:

- Non-teleological views, examining when and how things happen, but not why
- Phalanx themes, where people are members of the larger group and follow its rules and behaviors rather than acting as individuals
- The biblical story of Cain and Abel
- Social class
- Racism
- Gender inequality or misogyny (a hatred of women)

Non-teleological Theory. Steinbeck's interests in both non-teleological ideas and phalanx theories do not show themselves as strongly in this work as they do in some others (such as *The Grapes of Wrath*). However, the story depicts, quite strongly, the contrast between individuals and groups. George and Lennie's dream of owning a place of their own one day is unrealistic, since they are too poor. But the dream becomes more possible if they become part of a group, with Candy and Crooks.

More than this, however, is the contrast between the life of an individual and the life of a group.

The non-teleological view focuses not on what is right or wrong or good or evil. Instead, it argues that people or animals do what is necessary to survive. Things just are; there is no explanation. That this viewpoint affected Steinbeck's writing may be evident from the original title, *Something That Happened*. It is clear in the story that Lennie does not mean to cause harm. It just happens. In the telling of the story, no one emerges as the hero. Steinbeck does not presume that one person's actions are any better or worse than another's—they simply are. Steinbeck shows the reader what happened—the how and what—but does not explain why. He allows the reader to observe the events and make up his or her own mind. As a result, people have many different opinions about the work. A few of them are discussed below.

Cain and Abel. The story of Cain and Abel is one that Steinbeck would write about later in detail with his novel, *East of Eden*. However, in *Of Mice and Men*, themes from the biblical story are reflected in the characters of George and Lennie. Cain and Abel were the sons of Adam and Eve. While George and Lennie are not brothers, they grew up together. When Lennie's Aunt Clara died, he left with George. In the biblical story, Cain is jealous of Abel. After he kills Abel, Cain is banished to a life of wandering. While jealousy is not seen in *Of Mice and Men*, other elements of the biblical story are, such as the wandering life of a bindle stiff.

The biblical story takes place after humans have lost their innocence. In *Of Mice and Men*, Lennie is an innocent, childlike figure. Professor William Goldhurst writes that the story examines the biblical question of whether humans are destined to wander the earth alone or to take care of one another.[6] Loneliness is a recurring theme throughout the story. Nearly every character struggles with some type of loneliness or feelings of separation. The dream of the farm, which is like the Garden of Eden for the men, is one that will lessen feelings of loneliness for Candy and Crooks. They both wish to escape their current situations as outcasts, separate from the other workers.

Further, migrant workers are lonely men who wander from one job to the next. George and Lennie travel together. This is uncommon, and the other men question the relationship. Later, both Candy and Crooks express interest in joining George and Lennie when they buy their own land. This, Goldhurst writes, shows optimism and a possible reversal of the fate of Cain to wander alone.[7] As the story continues, however, aloneness seems to be a dominant theme. Crooks removes himself from the plan after Curley's wife reminds him of his place in a white society. George is left alone after Lennie dies, but there is still hope when he leaves with Slim.

Other elements in the book are religious or faith-based themes. Concepts relating to light and darkness are found throughout. Much of the story takes place in the dark, as the men gather in the bunkhouse at night and talk. Lennie's acts of killing occur during the day, but the final scene in the story takes place as the sun is setting. Lennie understands that what he did is wrong, even if unintentional. At the end, he asks George if he is going to give him "hell" for what he did. George understands what he needs to do to save Lennie from the wrath of the other men. His act may seem cruel, but as writer Lee Dacus points out, George acts out of love. It is a result of his "responsibility of life and death over Lennie—a responsibility of godlike awesomeness constituted of love...."[8] Caring for Lennie right up to the end is a responsibility that George takes seriously. He would rather have the burden of killing his friend than leave Lennie's fate to the mob of angry men.

Social Class. Throughout his life, Steinbeck had an interest in the worker. From his early days working at various jobs while attending college, to his interviewing migrant workers prior to writing *The Grapes of Wrath*, he had an interest in portraying real people.

During the Great Depression, many people traveled to find work. Bindle stiffs represented a class of people that many did not want to talk about. They lived unconventional lives and represented a variety of ethnic backgrounds. Not only did Steinbeck seek to portray migrant workers accurately, he also wanted to create a story that these people would be more likely to read.

His depiction has been both praised and criticized. The lives of bindle stiffs were ones of hardship. They worked long, hard hours and rarely had much to show for it. Regardless of how people felt about this segment of society, it existed. The life of the migrant worker was "something that happened" in American society, which some people do not want to read about or do not want their children reading about.

Racism. Steinbeck wove issues of racial tension into the story and created a strong character in Crooks. At a time when racial tensions were high, Crooks represented a man who was not a stereotypical African American to some people. Well-read and intelligent, Crooks is a sympathetic character. The story depicts him in a very real way. Crooks must live in the barn, alongside the animals, because the other men do not want to share the bunkhouse with him. His disability also sets him apart. However, the reader learns that Crooks owns many books. Through his conversation with Lennie, the reader learns that Crooks is intelligent. He has a full understanding of his own situation and Lennie's. He is understandably bitter, but he is also aware.

During his conversations with Lennie and later Candy, Crooks comes out of his comfort zone temporarily. He expresses interest in being a part of the farm plan, even offering to work for free. His extreme loneliness is evident, as is his desire to be with others who treat him as a man, not an animal relegated to the barn. His situation looks hopeful, but only temporarily.

Once Curley's wife shows up and threatens to blackmail him, he quickly retreats to his former self. He understands that a white woman only has to say that something happened between herself and a black man. An accusation, whether true or not, could get a black man jailed or lynched at that time. Crooks knows this, as do readers. This depiction of Crooks, even if a bitter character, is one of intelligence. The reader can sympathize with Crooks, not only for his lonely situation but for the hopelessness of it as well. Despite his positive traits, some readers object to the way Crooks is treated in the story, both as an African-American man and as someone with a disability.

Misogyny. There are two female characters in *Of Mice and Men*, and only one is seen "on stage." The first is Lennie's Aunt Clara. Lennie's childhood caregiver is mentioned mostly in passing. Lennie does not remember her when she is first mentioned. He refers to her as "a lady" who used to give him mice. She is described more toward the end of the story, shortly before George finds Lennie at the hiding place. Lennie "sees" her, and she scolds him for doing bad things and for being a burden to George. She is not depicted as a loving caregiver.

The other woman in the story is Curley's wife. While Aunt Clara has a name, Curley's wife is never named. Instead, she is called a tart, a bitch, and a range of other derogatory terms. She is the catalyst of Lennie's downfall, yet she has no name and is described by some critics as a woman who only wants sex. Her vanity over her soft hair makes her invite Lennie to touch it, which leads to her death. Because of her looks, actions, and desire to be famous, the men in the story do not treat her well. However, just like the main characters, she too has big dreams that do not come true.

Unlike most of the other characters, however, she loses not only her dreams, but also her life. While her actions with Lennie may not seem innocent, both she and the puppy are victims of Lennie's strength. Her life is sad in many ways. She is treated poorly by her controlling husband, the men do not like her, and the reader can sense, even before her death, that she will not find happiness.

Some critics of the book object to the portrayal of Curley's wife. The men use several slang terms when describing her. To some readers, this is a misogynistic portrayal; that is, it shows hatred toward women. However, their words and actions were "true to character," in that Steinbeck wrote the men saying things that were believable. This does not mean that all bindle stiffs hated women, but this particular group did not like Curley's wife.

It is also important to note the difference between the characters and the author. Even though accused of portraying misogynistic views, Steinbeck himself did not hate women. Unlike Lennie, he was raised surrounded by loving women. He had a close friendship with his younger sister, Mary. He also frequently acknowledged the support he received from the women in his personal life.

Literary Devices

Steinbeck enjoyed experimenting with form in his fiction. He approached this novel with a unique purpose, and he wanted the novel to read like a play. Although the story is not exactly in play format, his goal was that the story could be adapted easily to the stage or the screen. Both have since been done. He also wanted to attract "reluctant readers." Although this term did not exist at the time, Steinbeck wanted to write a story to attract people that might not otherwise read a novel.

Structure. The structure of the story is basic but effective. The opening and closing scenes occur in the same place, creating a circular effect. The reader learns that the two men are escaping a previous job where Lennie got in trouble with a girl. Each scene logically leads to the next. There is only one girl at the new job, and the events naturally unfold to lead Lennie to the exact spot where he unwittingly causes trouble one more time. Lennie's downfall is determined from the beginning and is foreshadowed by the death of Candy's dog.

Some critics praised Steinbeck's approach, while others did not. Overall, the story won critical acclaim after publication. In some ways, the story follows a formula, but as authors Jeffrey Schultz and Luchen Li write in *Critical Companion to John Steinbeck:* "He deliberately manipulates the reader, but so obviously that the manipulation is excusable."[9] Not everyone agrees with this, however. One of the earliest criticisms of the work condemned the work for being too mechanical. Mark Van Doren, literary editor for the *Nation*, wrote in 1937 that the story is mechanical and that the characters are subhuman.[10]

Setting. Steinbeck's use of setting is critical in the novel. Author John H. Timmerman writes: "The mountains that frame the story, as they frame the little thing that happened in the lives of George and Lennie, always carry large significance for Steinbeck."[11] They frame the opening and closing scenes as much as they frame the story at large. Timmerman writes of the symbolism in the setting at the close of the story and points out that "the darkening mountains represent the mystery of death, carefully sustained in the minor imagery of the heron seizing and eating the little water snakes."[12] In *Of Mice and Men*, Steinbeck limited the settings to accommodate the stage or screen. Even though the men spend most of their days working in the field, the story's middle scenes take place in the bunkhouse and in the barn, where conditions are rough. The men share close quarters and dirty living conditions. They talk, read, and play solitaire for entertainment.

Dialogue. Much of the story is presented in dialogue. The reader also learns much of the backstory through dialogue, such as when Lennie's Aunt Clara is introduced. Lennie talks about a lady he remembers, and

George reminds him that the lady was his Aunt Clara. George also tells Slim about their background, which the reader also "hears." Additionally, key plot points are shown through dialogue, such as when Candy says that he should have shot the dog. The

This picture of a migrant woman and her children was taken by the great photographer Dorothea Lange in 1936. Steinbeck's writing often featured characters on the margins of society.

words spoken by the men—both the vulgar terms and the uneducated slang—are a primary reason why the book has been continuously challenged since its first publication.

Symbolism. Steinbeck used symbolism in a variety of ways. One example is the symbolism of the mountains at the opening and closing of the story. The mountains are large, and George and Lennie are small in comparison. Even though the "something that happened" in their lives affected them personally, in the grand scheme of things, it is a small incident. The smallness of the men (and perhaps humanity) contrasts with the largeness of the mountains.

The ideas of solitude and unrealized dreams are also shown symbolically throughout the story. For example, most of the men travel alone, and though they have each other to talk to in the bunkhouse, they choose to play solitaire instead of card games together. When the men discuss their dreams, they realize that they might be able to reach their dreams working together. George and Lennie decide that Candy can join them on their farm. However, the reader understands that this will probably never happen. Curley's wife also represents solitude and unrealized dreams. She is the only woman in the story, and she is obviously lonely (although the men in the story do not understand this). She, too, is looking for "happily ever after," but gave up her dreams of going to Hollywood when she married Curley.

Other symbolism in the story, as in much of Steinbeck's work, appears to be based in Christian themes. Some critics have suggested, for example, that the dream of the farm represents Eden or heaven. The men's hope lies in the future.[13] Lee Dacus, in "Christian Symbolism in *Of Mice and Men*," argues that other Christian symbols are present throughout the story. He writes that Lennie is an innocent figure who unwittingly makes mistakes. George is a Christ figure, in that he is responsible for Lennie and protects him.[14] Dacus also writes of the strong theme of love throughout the story. Even though George kills Lennie, he acts out of love and caring. He knows that if he does not, Lennie's fate would be a cruel death or imprisonment. He knows that the men will not be kind to Lennie if they find him. George's act of killing is to spare Lennie any unnecessary pain.[15]

Critical Responses

Of Mice and Men sold very well. Although he did not relish fame, Steinbeck became even more famous after the publication of his sixth novel. Overall, both critics and the public praised the book, and they still do so today. As of March 2006, for example, nearly one thousand reviews on Amazon.com average a rating of 4.5 out of 5.0. Young readers wrote a number of those reviews.

Upon publication, most of the reviews were positive. Some called the book a masterpiece, a literary feat, and a great story.[16] Critical and academic readings of the work vary, depending on the approach of the critic. A feminist reading the book, for example, will have a much different response from someone reading it for its historical context. As with most literature, analysts offer differing opinions on the story's literary worth.

The language used in the book became a topic of discussion almost immediately upon publication. Mark Van Doren, in a negative review of the book in 1937, criticized the characters and their language. He argued that the characters do not understand even the most basic rules of conduct. He also wrote that "...the bunk house talk is terrific: God damn, Jesus Christ, what the hell, you crazy bastard, I gotta gut ache, and things like that. The dialect never varies, just as the story never runs uphill."[17]

In contrast, another critic, R. Ganapathy, took a much different view of the language used in the story. Ganapathy asserted that Steinbeck created a lyrical use of the language. "Certain powerfully racy and colloquial words and sentences, profane and shocking at times, are so artistically repeated over and over again that they sink into the reader's mind as refrains in a song."[18] Ganapathy compared the lyricism to a lullaby. The reader becomes used to the lyricism throughout the story and is lulled by it, which leads to a powerful ending. When George shoots Lennie, the men are discussing their dream of the farm, in the same comforting, rhythmical tones used throughout the book. This, Ganapathy claimed, makes it difficult for readers to come to grips with the "gruesome end. Our sympathies are already with Lennie, however bad and primitive he might be, and his death comes as a shock to us. Steinbeck does make us think here of the [mysteriousness] of life."[19]

Many analysts of Steinbeck's fiction write about his non-teleological viewpoint. *Of Mice and Men* is often discussed in this framework, because the "something that happened" is not explained in the sense of *why* it happened; it simply did. Steinbeck wrote most of his fiction from an observational standpoint, providing the reader with the evidence but not providing any judgments about the situation. That is left to the reader. This approach has also led to much debate among literary critics. Some praise the form, while others say that it leaves the work lacking necessary drama. Although people will probably never agree on what exactly makes great literature, these arguments point to some broader questions about literature, such as its purpose.

In writing about the non-teleological viewpoint, Richard Astro argues that Steinbeck's "uniquely delicate handling of his fictional materials"[20] is what makes the work excellent. He writes: "Steinbeck neither blames nor accuses in Of Mice and Men; he simply tells a story about the way in which 'the best laid schemes o' mice an' men gang aft a'gley.'"[21] He writes that Steinbeck uses non-teleological thinking as a fictional method. While doing so, he does not suggest that teleological views are not important. However, the non-teleological approach gives the writer distance from the characters to present them more fully. This, in turn, allows the reader to develop his or her own conclusions.

In contrast, some critics think that the story lacks necessary literary tragedy. Harry Thornton Moore authored the first critical study of Steinbeck in 1939. Of Steinbeck's characters, he writes: "It is disturbing to find so many of these likeable heroes going down so consistently in spiritual defeat or meeting with a brutal death."[22] He also writes, in reference to *Of Mice and Men*: "Violence without tragedy: that is the weakness of this book."[23] He argues that in the literary sense, there is no tragedy, which traditionally comes out of the character. He argues that Lennie is not tragic because too much is stacked against him to begin with. His fate is sealed from the beginning, which is not tragedy in the usual sense. Tragedy often occurs because, as a result of his or her own choices and actions, a character gets into a situation that he or she cannot escape. Lennie cannot control his actions, so there is no tragedy.

Moore argued that George is not a tragic figure, either. Tragic figures in literature often have a "tragic flaw," such as excessive pride, greed, or desire, which leads to their downfall. In this story, George's acts are the result of the situation, not something he brought upon himself (although it could be argued that his flaw is caring for Lennie). He kills Lennie to save Lennie from the others. In Moore's opinion, Lennie's death is a brutal shock to the reader, despite the tricks used throughout the story to prepare the reader for the ending, such as the parallel between the death of Candy's dog and Lennie's death.

Steinbeck's portrayal of George also shows the non-teleological viewpoint. The story shows the "what" and "how" of the situation, but does not attempt to answer "why." Traditionally, in classic literature, a tragic flaw or mistake provides the answer to why characters act the way they do, with tragic results. In Shakespeare's *Hamlet*, for example, the main character is indecisive over doing his duty and killing the uncle who has murdered Hamlet's father. His hesitancy leads to the deaths of many innocent people—Hamlet's mother, his girlfriend, her brother—and eventually to the death of Hamlet himself. By contrast, in *Of Mice and Men*, George's actions are caused by circumstances, not by a flaw in his character.

Despite some criticisms, most critics consider the book a classic in American literature. Its experimental, short form makes it easily readable and a good choice for high school classes. Authors Jeffrey Schultz and Luchen Li write: "*Of Mice and Men* continues to be required reading for many high school advanced place-ment English literature courses. In this sense, it has become an American classic, still analyzed and debated in American classrooms."[24] It is a study of literary form and presents issues for discussion about American history, racial prejudices, and social, gender, and moral issues.

Chapter 5

The Grapes of Wrath

Many people consider *The Grapes of Wrath* to be Steinbeck's greatest work. Published in 1939, two years after *Of Mice and Men*, it follows the Joad family as they struggle to make a living following the 1930s Dust Bowl. A number of factors negatively affected farmers throughout the Midwest and Southwest. These included a severe and lasting drought and farmers' reliance on banks for financial support. When the Great Depression hit the country in 1929, these factors left many farmers destitute and homeless. Word that work could be found in California spread throughout the country. Thousands of people migrated west in search of the American Dream and a better life.

Steinbeck's work researching migratory workers and his interest in the worker prompted him to write about the struggles faced by thousands of people. He wanted to bring greater awareness to the issue. While writing the book, Steinbeck kept a journal that he used to warm up before working on the novel. It was published in 1989 as *Working Days: The Journals of The Grapes of Wrath*, edited by Robert DeMott.

Plot Summary

The novel opens with a narrative summary of the drought. Tom Joad is returning home. He has just been paroled from prison after serving a four-year sentence for killing a man in self-defense. He meets Jim Casy, who used to be a preacher. Casy tells Tom that the banks have repossessed the farms, leaving many families homeless. Tom and Casy walk to Tom's Uncle John's home, where they find the family. This includes Tom's Uncle John, father Tom (Pa Joad), mother (Ma Joad), Granma and Grandpa, and Tom's siblings Noah, Al, Rose of Sharon (also called Rosasharn, who is pregnant and married to Connie), Ruthie, and Winfield.

The family leaves to go to California to look for jobs; Casy joins them. Theirs is one of many vehicles traveling along the road. When they stop for the night alongside the highway, they meet the Wilsons. Grandpa suffers a stroke and dies. The men dig a grave near the highway and bury him. Al fixes the Wilsons' car, and the two families agree to travel together. When they finally reach the California border, they hear about the situation in California. They also learn that the locals refer to the people traveling as "Okies," a derogatory name for people migrating west.

Pa and Tom decide that the family should continue traveling that night. Noah leaves the family. The Wilsons stay behind because Mrs. Wilson is dying. The Joads cross the desert overnight and reach a green valley. Ma tells the family that Granma died during the night. They spend the last of their money to bury her. The Joads stop at a crowded camp. Tom and

This shows a scene from the movie version of *The Grapes of Wrath*, starring Henry Fonda (at left) as Tom Joad.

Casy get into a scuffle with the police, and Casy is arrested. Connie leaves to return home. The remaining family moves to a government-run camp. As they go, they see the police burning the camp they just left. The new camp has organizing committees, running water, and toilets. Tom learns of some work, which turns out to pay much less than expected. He speaks to a farmer, who tells him that workers are planning to riot during an upcoming dance at the camp. At the dance, a group of men are caught trying to start a fight. They admit that the Growers Association paid them to start trouble.

The Joads head north to find more work. They cross a picket line to work. Everyone works, and they earn a dollar. Tom goes for a walk and finds Casy, who has been released from jail. Casy tells Tom that the men are on strike. When the strike is over, the farmer will reduce wages even more. Casy tells Tom why it is important that the workers fight together. As individuals, they will not have any impact, but as a unified group, they can. Police raid the strike, and Casy is killed. Tom then kills the man who attacked Casy.

The family leaves the next day. They stay in an old boxcar with another family, the Wainwrights, while Tom hides in the woods. Ruthie brags to some other children that Tom killed a man, so Ma tells Tom he has to leave. Tom has been thinking about what Casy said about the strike. He wants to organize the people and continue Casy's work.

Heavy rains fall, and the river rises, threatening the boxcars. Rose of Sharon gets a chill and goes into labor. The baby is stillborn. Uncle John places the baby in an apple box and floats it downstream. The family leaves to find a dry shelter. They meet a boy and his father, who is dying from starvation. Rose of Sharon offers the dying man milk from her breast.

Primary Characters

Once again, Steinbeck focused on workers facing nearly insurmountable odds. The situations depicted in the book highlight a situation that thousands of migrant workers faced. However, humanity is made of individuals, and Steinbeck included some strong personalities in his novel. The following is an overview of the primary characters.

Tom Joad. Tom is the first main character introduced in the novel. He is hitchhiking home after being released from prison, where he served time for killing a man in self-defense. He is a significant character throughout the novel. While he is somewhat of a drifter in the beginning, he helps his family along their journey to California. He later decides to help the cause of the migrant workers.

Tom Joad is the male protagonist of the story, and even though the novel is told from an omniscient third-person point of view, in many ways, the story is Tom's story. He changes throughout the story from worrying only about his family to being concerned about everyone in his family's position. However, he is also a violent character, which some readers find offensive. Before the novel begins, Tom has served time for killing a man. Later in the book, he brutally kills Casy's killer with a club.

Jim Casy. Jim Casy, a former preacher, meets Tom Joad at the beginning of the novel. He travels with the Joads to California. Throughout the story, he is in a bit of limbo. He is unsure of his purpose, but knows he wants to help others. Grateful to the Joads for allowing him to travel with them, he saves Tom from going to prison again. Once Casy is released, he goes on strike with the migrant workers. He is killed in a scuffle with the police during a raid on a strike.

Even though Casy is a *former* preacher (and Casy makes this point repeatedly in the story), he uses profanity throughout the novel, just as many other characters do. For example, when he meets Tom Joad again toward the end of the story, their greeting is one that many people might find offensive:

> "Casy!" Tom cried. "Casy! For Chris' sake, what you doin' here?"
>
> "Why, my God, it's Tom Joad! Come on in, Tommy. Come on in."
>
> "Know him, do ya?" the man in front asked.

"Know him? Christ, yes. Knowed him for years. I come west with him."[1]

Pa Joad (Old Tom). Pa Joad is the head of the family. He, along with the other men (excluding Grandpa Joad) makes the decision to leave for California. He sees the flyers announcing work and decides that it is the best course for his family. As the trip and the novel progress, however, Pa loses control over his struggling family. In a standoff with Ma Joad on the road, he loses an argument about separating the family. From this point on, Pa becomes more disheartened about the family's situation, and Ma accuses him of not fulfilling his role as the head of the family.

Ma Joad. Ma Joad is the center of the family, who tries to keep everyone together. She loses faith as she sees her family falling apart, with the deaths of Grandpa and Granma, Noah's leaving, and later Connie's departure. However, she maintains her resolve throughout and emerges as the head of the family by the end of the story. It is her suggestion that Rose of Sharon feed the dying man. She knows the importance of the whole, including the family unit and the larger human family.

Ma Joad is also the first family member to witness the discrimination against traveling families. When the family stops in California, Ma encounters a police officer. He asks her who is with her and what the family

80

The Grapes of Wrath

plans to do. Ma tells him that where she comes from, men treat women with respect:

> The man took two steps backward. "Well, you ain't in your country now. You're in California, an' we don't want you goddamn Okies settlin' down."
>
> Ma's advance stopped. She looked puzzled. "Okies?" she said softly. "Okies."
>
> "Yeah, Okies! An' if you're here when I come tommorra, I'll run ya in." He turned and walked to the next tent and banged on the canvas with his hand.
>
> "Who's in there?" he asked.
>
> Ma went slowly back under the tarpaulin. She put the skillet in the utensil box. She sat down slowly. Rose of Sharon watched her secretly. And when she saw Ma fighting with her face, Rose of Sharon closed her eyes and pretended to sleep.[2]

This scene marks the beginning of the family's struggle against discrimination. They move several times because the locals do not want "their kind" in California. It is also an example of profanity used throughout the book.

81

Grandpa and Granma Joad. Grandpa Joad does not want to go on the journey. The family puts medicine in his coffee; when he falls asleep, they put him in the truck. He dies the first night. Granma Joad falls ill shortly after. Ma Joad watches over her body as the family travels through the California desert. They bury Granma in Bakersfield.

Noah Joad. Noah is the oldest son. He is a strange man, and along the way to California, leaves the family to live as a hermit. True to his name, he leaves at a river, before the family crosses the desert in California.

Al Joad. Al is the third son of the family. He is an accomplished mechanic, and he helps the family and the Wilsons reach California. Toward the end of the story, he, too, leaves the family, to marry Aggie Wainwright.

Rose of Sharon (Rosasharn). Rose of Sharon is the oldest Joad daughter. She is pregnant and worries throughout the journey about the health of her baby. She is married to Connie Rivers, who eventually leaves the family. As foreshadowed throughout the book, her baby is still-born. However, she offers her breast milk to a starving man at the end of the story, demonstrating her maturity and willingness to give and to look outside of herself. Some people who oppose the book find her act of offering her breast milk to a grown man offensive, even though the man is starving.

Connie Rivers. Connie is Rose of Sharon's husband. He has dreams of working in a factory or in radio repair. As the situation worsens, he becomes increasingly angry that he did not stay behind and take a job driving a tractor. He leaves his pregnant wife and her family.

Ruthie and Winfield Joad. Ruthie, age twelve, and Winfield, age ten, are the youngest Joad children. Winfield becomes ill during the journey and almost dies. Ruthie is stubborn and self-absorbed. She tells some other children that Tom is on parole for killing a man, which forces Tom to go into hiding.

Uncle John. Uncle John is Pa Joad's brother. He blames himself for his wife's death and believes that he is the cause of bad luck. At one point, he leaves the family to go drinking, using some money he has been hiding. When Rose of Sharon's baby is born dead, he places the baby in a box and places it in the river, which parallels the biblical story of Moses.

The Wilsons. The Wilsons travel with the Joads for the middle part of the journey. They provide a place for Grandpa Joad when he falls ill and dies. When Mrs. Wilson becomes too ill to continue, they stay behind.

Themes
Multiple themes run through *The Grapes of Wrath*:

The American Dream. Perhaps one of the most obvious themes in the book is the family's desire for something better. As their predecessors did before them, they travel west in search of a better life. Many people are never able to realize the American Dream. In the story, this is true for the Joads and thousands of other families as well.

The search for the American Dream leaves the family disappointed. However, they maintain a sense of faith and hope at the end of the story. When Rose of Sharon offers her breast milk, this act shows a hope for the future and demonstrates that life goes on. The reader has a sense that the family will continue traveling and find some source of comfort and stability.

Family. Family is a very strong theme throughout the book. As the trip unravels, so, too, do parts of the family. At first, Ma Joad's resolve keeps the remaining family together. She does her best to maintain the family unit throughout the rest of the story, even though some family members die and some leave. The family represents a smaller version of the phalanx. As individuals, more family members likely would perish. As a unit, they find strength in each other and help one another through the trials of their situation. Ma Joad is the central family figure. She fights hard to keep the individuals in the group.

Families helping each other is also a central theme. Throughout the story, families are mostly courteous to one another. After the Wilsons help the Joads

84

when Grampa dies, the Joads return the favor by traveling together, sharing supplies, and helping to repair the Wilsons' car. Along the road, families camp by the roadside. They understand that they are all in the same situation. These families share a common bond, which Ma acknowledges when the men talk about splitting up after the Wilsons' car breaks down.

> The eyes of the whole family shifted back to Ma. She was the power. She had taken control. "The money we'd make wouldn't do no good," she said. "All we got is the family unbroke. Like a bunch of cows, when the lobos are ranging, stick all together. I ain't scared while we're all here, all that's alive, but I ain't gonna see us bust up. The Wilsons here is with us, an' the preacher is with us. I can't say nothin' if they want to go, but I'm a-goin' cat-wild with this here piece of bar-arn if my own folks busts up." Her tone was cold and final.[3]

At the end of the story, the Joads and Wainwrights help each other survive in the boxcar, and Rose of Sharon helps another family in need.

Social and Working Conditions. When Steinbeck reported on the conditions that migrant workers lived and worked in, he developed a desire to write honestly about their situation. His decision made him very unpopular with some groups, such as the Associated

Farmers. However, he did his best to portray the situation accurately using the fictional Joad family. Prior to writing the work, he interviewed many migrant workers and lived among them for a time. Through this process, he heard many stories. He also visited a government camp such as the one in the book.

Steinbeck showed the problem that happens when there are too many workers and too little work. Those in control, the farmers, lowered wages further and further because as workers grew more desperate for work, they would take anything, no matter how unfair the wage. The strikes and movement toward unions at the end of the novel were the result of unfair working practices. Because Steinbeck did not write about a glorious America, some people criticized him for being a Marxist or Socialist. He was neither. He saw himself as simply reporting on an important situation, using a fictional platform.

Phalanx Theory. Steinbeck's phalanx theory is evident throughout the novel. The theory is that individuals are a part of a larger whole. The larger whole has a life of its own. Each Joad is a member of the larger family. The family is one element of a much larger group of struggling families. The individual worker is not as effective as a group of unified workers. Every individual is part of the larger group of humanity. This is clearly demonstrated at the end when Rose of Sharon moves past her personal grief over losing her baby and offers her breast milk to help another human being. Throughout the novel, the phalanx concept reaches multiple levels.

Faith. The concept of faith comes up throughout the novel in various forms. This includes everything from religious faith to blind faith that something better will come along eventually. Casy questions his faith and direction throughout the story. He ultimately finds his purpose in helping others—not through religion, but by helping the workers organize. Granma Joad has ongoing faith in her religion and asks Casy to pray for her and the family. Ma Joad's faith lies in her family and the need to keep it together as much as possible. Rose of Sharon shows her faith in the future by offering her milk at the close of the story. Different characters define faith in different ways, but the concept is evident throughout.

Literary Devices

In *The Grapes of Wrath*, Steinbeck used a variety of literary devices to achieve his ends.

Form. As with other works, Steinbeck experimented with the form of the novel, using alternating chapters. One set of chapters provides the story of the Joad family. The other chapters present a broader view of the situation, such as the Dust Bowl, the migration of thousands of workers to California, the Great Depression, and the plight of migrant workers.

Steinbeck also experiments with form within the alternating chapters. Even though these chapters provide an overview, they often use specific details and dialogue, giving life to the people in these scenes. However, the chapters use a "stream of consciousness" format, where the narrator "talks" continuously, with little formal structure. There is no punctuation to show the dialogue, for example. Additionally, the chapters do not form as logical a story line as the Joad chapters do. They are easy to follow, though, as they complement the Joad story. Each scene takes place along the travels of the Joads, providing a broader perspective than that in the Joad chapters.

Point of View. The term *point of view* in writing refers to the perspective from which a story is told. Fiction is usually told in first- or third-person point of view. In a first-person narrative, a character tells the story using *I*. When using this method, the author can write only about things that the individual can see. A third-person point of view is told by an outside narrator and uses words such as *he, she,* and *they.* How much a narrator knows in the third-person point of view can vary. A narrator who knows what is going on all the time in all the characters' minds is called omniscient. Sometimes, however, a third-person narrator tells the story from one character's point of view. This is called limited omniscient.

In *The Grapes of Wrath*, the chapters alternate between an all-knowing narrator in the chapters that inform the reader about the overall situation and a limited omniscient narrator who tells the story from the Joads' point of view. Steinbeck does not follow one character exclusively, but the family as a whole.

In using alternating chapters, Steinbeck allowed himself to step beyond the limited point of view of the Joad family. For example, the Joad family can see that there are many other families traveling west. In the alternating chapters, however, the reader learns through other people and events that the problem is much bigger than what the Joads can see on the road.

In applying his theories about non-teleological thinking and the phalanx through his narrative method, Steinbeck was able to present both the individual side of the story as well as the larger societal view of the story. He accomplished much more using this approach than he would have if he had limited himself to telling only the Joads' story. Of course, the Joads also represent the greater whole, as they are one family among thousands who find themselves homeless, out of work, and desperate.

Setting. Steinbeck uses setting purposefully throughout all of his works. *The Grapes of Wrath* contains many examples. Before the family leaves, the local farms are dry and deserted, creating an eerie feeling and foreshadowing the difficult times ahead. The road is long and desolate, with a promised land at the end of the journey. As the Joads cross the desert at the end, they see a glorious, luscious green valley. This "Eden" is short-lived, as the family soon faces the harsh reality of the situation. Granma has died, and the camps are as desolate as the Joads feel. Fruits are growing around them, but they are not allowed to take any, even though they are starving. To fuel the workers' anger, the farmers destroy crops and leave huge amounts of fruit to go to waste, even though thousands of starving people are right there in the camps. Again, they can see "Eden"— the fruit trees—but cannot enter. Because Steinbeck included such scenes, the Associated Farmers of Kern County (California) banned the book in 1939 shortly after its release, claiming that the book was derogatory toward the state.[4]

Toward the end, the Joads are stuck in the boxcar with an oncoming flood, as the rain is heavy. Much in the way that the biblical flood represented the beginning of a new world, this, too, seems true for the Joads. They leave the boxcar, only to later help a dying man. This indicates that there is hope for the future and that things will start to look better now. They are still amid the flood, but they have now found dry ground and a new hope.

Symbolism. As with Steinbeck's other works, symbolism throughout the story sheds light on the larger issues. For example, writer Lee Burress points out the differences between animals and machines throughout the story: "Generally, the animal references stand for life and the references to machinery stand for depersonalized, inanimate ways of dealing with human problems."[5] The destructive tractors do the work previously done by farmers' animals, and they are used to bulldoze abandoned farmhouses. And while animals represent life and perseverance, Steinbeck uses symbolic action to show frustration and irony, such as in the following scene, when the family is driving to a farm to work:

Mr. and Mrs. Frank Pipkin and musicians are recorded performing old ballads in 1941. Mrs. Pipkin is believed by many to be the model for Ma Joad.

A snake wriggled across the warm highway. Al zipped over and ran it down and came back to his own lane.

"Gopher snake," said Tom. "You oughtn't to done that."

"I hate 'em," said Al gaily. "Hate all kinds. Give me the stomach-quake."[6]

Al's action of killing the harmless gopher snake parallels the way the farm owners and authorities in California treat the "Okies." Just as Al hates all snakes, regardless of whether or not they pose any real threat, so, too, do many people in California hate all migrant families.

Critical Responses

Many consider *The Grapes of Wrath* to be Steinbeck's greatest work. It was a best seller, and though it faced some criticism, the overall reception was positive. However, some responses were negative. In St. Louis, Missouri, after three copies were ordered burned for vulgar language, the library moved the books to a shelf labeled "for adults only."[7] Also upon publication, people in Kern County, California, banned the novel, a move initiated by the Associated Farmers. However, some migrant workers who read the work said that it was an accurate description of their lives. Still, the novel created a range of controversy because it criticized an aspect of American life. Jeffrey Schultz and Luchen Li write that Steinbeck's "reaction to the controversy was not only outrage and extended depression, but a growing fear of completing another novel, which he did not attempt for several years afterward."[8]

The book was the third of three novels that dealt with labor issues. Steinbeck developed a reputation as a writer for the lower class, but he later moved away from this. Once again, some praised his branching out, while others did not. In many ways, no matter what Steinbeck did, someone criticized him. However, he loved writing and wanted to experiment with as many different forms as possible. This resulted in different directions following *The Grapes of Wrath*. However, his departure from this approach to writing added to the belief that this was his greatest work. The novel won Steinbeck the Pulitzer Prize in 1939, but that did not prevent critical reviews.

J. P. Hunter wrote in the early 1960s that since the book's publication, it had received "increasingly harsh reviews" throughout the years.[9] The criticisms included "lack of character development, imperfect conception of structure, careless working out of theme, and sentimentality."[10] Hunter argues that the criticisms are not justified. For example, while others criticized the final scene in *The Grapes of Wrath* for being a sensational act, Hunter writes that it represents a key shift. Until that time, Rose of Sharon's main concerns were for herself, Connie, and the unborn child. However, her act of selflessness symbolizes a change, or a new order.[11] Hunter contends that the final scenes of the novel "demonstrate a careful working out of theme in fictional terms."[12] That is, the final scenes do not unravel, as other critics claimed, but instead present a careful shift in viewpoint. The Joads move from a position of seeing only their own problems to understanding the problem as it affects many. As the family makes this shift, the bigger picture shown through the narrative chapters parallel the broad understanding obtained by the family. For example, Tom decides he wants to organize the workers. Alone, each worker cannot do much, but as a group, they might be able to change things.

Hunter noted that Steinbeck developed the novel using biblical elements as a background. Others have also remarked on Steinbeck's use of Christian symbolism throughout the novel. Some see Casy as a Christ figure. Much as Christ went away to meditate, so does Casy. Following this period, Casy knows what he needs to do to help others. He helps organize the workers, and dies as a result. The California valley represents Eden, yet the Joads (and many others) cannot enter. Uncle John's sending the dead baby floating down the river is a dark contrast to Moses being sent down the river. While Moses later returned to set his people free, the Joads see no freedom ahead. However, Rose of Sharon makes a sacrifice at the end of the book, giving of herself so that another may live. All of these ideas are reminiscent of biblical themes.

Another issue that stands out among critics and readers alike is Steinbeck's depiction of women in this novel. While he has been criticized elsewhere for negative depictions of women, this book contains a very positive and strong depiction of a woman in Ma Joad. She is the glue that holds the family together. Without her, the family would likely suffer and fall apart much more than it does. She is a strong and realistic character. Rose of Sharon also is a positive role model at the story's end.

Since the publication of the novel, some critics have questioned whether the book is art or propaganda. When the novel came out, the issues with migrant workers were prevalent. Some viewed the novel as simple propaganda, a story written to expose the plight of the California workforce. Others see the novel as a great American classic, exploring an aspect of American history. Those questioning the art of the work analyze literary elements such as plot, structure, and characterization. Critics disagree on the novel's merits in these areas. Some claim that Steinbeck wrote a brilliant novel, while others claim the story is seriously lacking.

In analyzing the question of art versus propaganda, B. R. McElderry, Jr., writes that literary immortality may be impossible in modern times, due to the large numbers of books published every year. However, he also writes that "if classics are to emerge from the first forty years of this century, I can think of not more than a dozen novels in America that are so likely or such fit candidates for that measure of immortality."[13] *The Grapes of Wrath* is one of McElderry's candidates.

Will the book continue to be used in the curriculum in the twenty-first century? This partly depends on trends. In recent years, books dealing with the self and personal identity have been used frequently. However, as Barbara A. Heavilin observed, educators are interested in material that shows emotional intelligence and empathy, or the ability to understand and relate to the struggles of others. She notes that educators understand that humans are complex creatures whose abilities depend on heart and soul as well as intellect.... Steinbeck knows all of this most passionately with his own heart, mind, and soul, and the book will probably continue to resonate in the minds and souls of readers for generations to come.[14]

Chapter 6

East of Eden

Of Mice and Men and *The Grapes of Wrath* are Steinbeck's most often banned or challenged books because they are the ones most often used in the school curriculum. However, *East of Eden*, published in 1952, makes these lists as well. While the other two works are often singled out for the bad language, this work includes more blatant sexual references and violence. As with the other works, *East of Eden* was not written specifically for young readers. While it is a classic and a book that Steinbeck was pleased with, it is debatable whether children should read it. *East of Eden* is a longer work that depicts an epic tale about the lives of two families. It deals with difficult and mature topics. Steinbeck devoted a great deal of emotional energy to creating the book. The story incorporates much of Steinbeck's personal family history, and he wrote it in part as a gift to his sons.

East of Eden was Steinbeck's twelfth and longest novel. It was an instant best seller. A few years later, in

1955, a movie depicting part of the story was made starring James Dean. Some view *East of Eden* as Steinbeck's greatest work. It is very different from his earlier, well-known novels, such as *The Grapes of Wrath*. Some people welcomed the change. Others wished for a return to his earlier style. However, Steinbeck did not set out to please others. He wanted to apply everything he had learned about writing to that point and put it into one novel. More than in any of his other books, the narrator in *East of Eden* reflects Steinbeck's views. As a result, the novel has more of an inward focus than his previous novels.

Plot Summary

East of Eden follows two families, the Trasks and the Hamiltons. The story opens with a description of the Salinas Valley, followed by the introduction of Samuel Hamilton and his wife, who have nine children. The reader also meets the Trask family. The two main Trask characters are brothers Adam and Charles. Their father, Cyrus Trask, favors Adam, who leaves to serve the military and later returns to the family farm. Meanwhile, Charles learns that their father has died and left the brothers a large inheritance. The reader then meets Cathy Ames, later known as Kate, who is primarily an evil character. The brothers Adam and Charles find her after she has been beaten nearly to death. They nurse her back to health. Cathy marries Adam, and Charles is jealous.

Adam and Cathy move to the Salinas Valley. Adam employs a Chinese cook, Lee, who meets and befriends Samuel Hamilton. Meanwhile, the Hamilton children have grown; one of them, Olive, becomes a teacher. Cathy attempts to abort a pregnancy and nearly dies. Adam forces her to continue with the pregnancy. Cathy delivers twin boys, shoots Adam, and leaves. Adam survives, but is devastated. Samuel later tells Adam that Cathy is a prostitute in Salinas and has changed her name to Kate. She tricks and murders the owner of the whorehouse and inherits the business. Adam becomes severely withdrawn, and Lee takes care of the twins, Aron and Caleb (Cal). After Samuel Hamilton dies, Adam goes to Salinas to find Kate. He confronts her, and she tells him that his brother Charles is father to one of the twins. Seeing Kate for what she really is, Adam finally overcomes his attachment to her. Adam moves the family to Salinas. He also tries to contact his brother, Charles, now ten years since they last spoke. He learns that Charles has died and left a large amount of money to Adam and his wife. Adam decides to tell Kate about the money. Cal learns the truth about their mother when he overhears Adam and Lee talking about her.

Adam loses a lot of money in a failed business venture. Cal goes to see his mother, and gains a better understanding of his father. He later tells Adam that he knows about Kate. Aron leaves for college, and Cal earns some money by gambling on bean prices. Cal figures out that Adam has always favored Aron because he

John Steinbeck poses with copies of his books. He experimented with many different forms in fiction.

looks like their mother. On Thanksgiving, Cal tries to give Adam the money he has earned. Adam refuses the money. Cal takes Aron to the whorehouse, where they meet Kate. The morning after Aron learns the truth about his mother, he leaves for the army without telling anyone. Kate commits suicide after her past actions catch up to her. She leaves everything to Aron. Cal burns the money he tried to give to his father. The family learns that Aron died in the war. Upon hearing the news, Adam suffers a stroke. Cal feels guilty over what he has done. Lee takes him to Adam's bed, where Adam struggles to give his son his blessing, raising his hand and whispering *timshel*. This is a biblical term that, according to Lee, means that people can choose to overcome sin.

Selected Characters

Steinbeck used the biblical story of Cain and Abel as a backdrop to the story, but he did not replicate the biblical characters. Instead, he used elements from the biblical characters and added individual characteristics. In addition, the Hamilton family is based on Steinbeck's maternal family, and their story is real to the extent that Steinbeck knew and remembered (he was three years old when Samuel Hamilton died). The following is an overview of the primary characters in the story.

Cyrus Trask. Cyrus Trask is the father of Adam and Charles Trask. He is a manipulative military man and strict father. He favors Adam, and sends him to war to learn to become a man. When he dies, he leaves a large fortune to his sons.

Adam Trask. Adam Trask is one of the story's main characters. He is favored by his father, which makes his brother Charles jealous. They both fall in love with the same woman, Cathy Ames. Adam marries her and they move to Salinas. Cathy gives birth to twin boys and leaves Adam. He finally gets over his obsession with her. He raises his two sons, Cal and Aron, with the help of his Chinese cook, Lee. When Aron is killed in combat, Adam suffers a stroke. At the end of the story, he gives Cal his blessing by uttering the word *timshel.*

Charles Trask. Charles is Adam's brother. He is jealous of Adam because their father favors him. At one point, he tries to kill Adam. He is the father of one of the twins (they were not identical).

Cathy (Kate) Ames. Cathy is Adam Trask's wife. She leaves him to become a prostitute after giving birth to sons Cal and Aron. She later tells Adam that his brother, Charles, is the father of one of the boys. After a life of lies and destruction, she commits suicide, leaving all her money to Aron.

Samuel Hamilton. Samuel Hamilton is based on John Steinbeck's maternal grandfather, Samuel. His story, along with that of the other Hamiltons, is based on Steinbeck's personal history. In the story, Samuel helps

102

deliver the Trask boys and develops a lasting friendship with Adam Trask's cook, Lee. He and Lee discuss religion and philosophy. Samuel runs his farm and is an inventor, but does not make much money with either.

Olive Hamilton. Olive Hamilton is the youngest of nine Hamilton children. She is based on Steinbeck's mother. At eighteen years of age, she becomes a teacher, working in a one-room schoolhouse.

Hamilton Family. The Hamilton family is based on Steinbeck's family. They are inspired by, and named after, Steinbeck's real family. The novel serves in part as a family history for Steinbeck's own sons, Thom and John.

Lee. Lee is Adam Trask's Chinese cook. For the first ten years of their lives, he is the primary caregiver of the Trask boys. He stays with the family throughout his life. He also befriends Samuel Hamilton. He serves as a philosopher and mother figure, helping to guide the family. Lee introduces Adam and Samuel to the concept of *timshel.* Lee had studied the book of Genesis, particularly the story of Cain and Abel. He finds that different versions of the Bible present two different ideas of overcoming sin. The King James version implies that "it was a promise that Cain would conquer sin"[1] through the words "thou shalt." However, Cain does not conquer sin. The American Standard Bible uses the words "do thou," which Lee says is not a promise, but an order.[2] He wonders why these two versions are so different, and investigates the original Hebrew word, *timshel*. Lee determines that it means "thou mayest." In this translation, Cain has the *choice* to overcome sin. This translation of the word refers to the idea of free will, where people can choose and determine how they will act.

Caleb (Cal) Trask. Cal is the more mischievous of the two Trask boys. He struggles with the good and evil within himself. He realizes from an early age that his father, Adam, favors Aron. Cal takes Aron to meet their mother. Aron does not want to accept that his mother runs a whorehouse, and he leaves for the army without telling anyone. He dies in combat, after which Adam suffers a stroke. Cal feels responsible for what has happened to his brother and father. Adam gives Cal his blessing in the last scene of the novel. (In the story of Cain and Abel, Cain kills Abel.)

Aron Trask. Aron Trask is favored by his father, Adam. He is innocent and pure, not wanting to recognize the evil in the world and in himself. This is especially obvious when he learns the truth about his mother. Unable to cope with the truth of who she is and where he comes from, he escapes the family by enlisting in the army, and he dies in battle.

Narrator. While the narrator is not technically a character in the story, he is an important element. In many ways, the narrator is Steinbeck himself. He refers to his home in the Salinas Valley and to the Hamiltons as his family. For example, early paragraphs in Chapter 1 begin with "I remember ..."[3] Steinbeck includes his own family history by including the Hamiltons in the story. The Trask family is fictional, and therefore Samuel Hamilton's interactions with that family are fictional as well. However, parts of the story are based on family stories that Steinbeck heard growing up.

The narrator is also an important figure because he comments on ideas of good and evil. For example, in the fourth part of the novel, the narrator states that all life centers around a struggle between good and evil. He says that good is immortal, while evil must continually be reborn. These ideas are seen throughout the story.

Themes

Stories from the Book of Genesis in the Bible are widespread throughout the novel, from the book's title to specific stories within Genesis. One of the most obvious and most often analyzed themes throughout the book is the parallel to the biblical story of Cain and Abel. Cain and Abel are the sons of Adam and Eve. Cain, feeling that God favors Abel, kills his brother and is banished from Eden. Adam is named after the biblical character, but he parallels Abel in the Cain and Abel story. He is favored by his father, and his brother Charles attempts to kill him. Later, Cal feels responsible for Aron's death.

Both sets of Trask brothers are named with the letters *C* and *A*, which are also combined in Cathy

Ames's name. Cathy is an evil force throughout the book, tempting others and committing sinful acts. The fictional story does not follow the biblical story exactly, but it draws on many religious themes throughout. These include good and evil, sin, lying, redemption, and forgiveness.

Parental rejection is another theme throughout the book. Cyrus favors his son Adam over Charles. This causes a great deal of conflict between the brothers. Even though Adam almost loses his life at the hands of Charles, he repeats the actions with his own sons. Adam favors Aron, which later leads to the family's destruction. Adam realizes at the end of the story that he is largely responsible for the events that have taken place, and he forgives his son, Cal.

Free will is another running theme throughout the story. The idea is expressed through the word *timshel*, a Hebrew word. The character Lee states that the word is translated incorrectly in the Bible. He argues that it means "thou mayest," which gives people a choice between good and evil. The Bible translations usually interpret it to mean "thou shalt" or "do thou," which are promises and commands rather than choices. At the close of the book, Adam's last word is *timshel*. The authors of the *Critical Companion to John Steinbeck* write: "In Steinbeck's belief, it is individual responsibility that invents moral conscience. The great asset of any society and human civilization as a whole is the talent and energy of its people."[4] Adam forgives his son (and perhaps himself) and grants his son free will to choose another path. In other words, Cal struggles with the good and evil within himself; he has the power to choose good and change his destiny.

Literary Devices

As in his other books, Steinbeck made use of a number of literary devices in *East of Eden*.

Setting. The novel opens with a description of the beautiful landscape of the Salinas Valley, surrounded by two mountains on either side. One is dark, and the other is light. Additionally, the Salinas Valley has areas with rich, fertile soil, as well as areas with dry, rocky soil. The fertile areas are similar to those of Eden, but they must be cultivated. In Eden, Adam and Eve did not have to grow food. Once Adam was banished from Eden, however, he had to "cultivate the soil from which they had been formed."[5] The east side of Eden is important because that is where God put a flaming sword that "turned in all directions" to "keep anyone from coming near the tree that gives life."[6] Adam Trask's land in the story *East of Eden* is green and lush, much like the land of Eden. The Hamiltons, who try to make do with much harder soil, struggle continually. Adam does nothing with his high-quality land.

The area east of Eden is also important to the story of Cain and Abel. After Cain kills Abel, God puts a mark on Cain as a warning that anyone who tries to kill Cain will be met with revenge. At this point, "Cain went away from the Lord's presence and lived in a land called

'Wandering,' which is east of Eden."[7] The area east of Eden is also translated as Nod in the King James translation of the Bible, which reads, "And Cain went out from the presence of the Lord, and dwelt in the land of Nod, on the east of Eden."[8]

Mixing Genres. East of Eden is a combination of fiction, nonfiction, and personal essay. In his earlier works, Steinbeck preferred to use the voice of an external narrator who observed the events of the story. In this story, Steinbeck is the narrator of the tale. He draws from and includes real characters from his own family and uses family stories. However, these real characters interact with the fictional Trask family. This approach was another Steinbeck experiment, and some critics claim that *East of Eden* is Steinbeck's greatest accomplishment. Schultz and Li write: "Scholars and literary analysts of Steinbeck's works . . . have taken Steinbeck's self-professed description of the book as his masterpiece seriously."[9]

Irony. Steinbeck uses irony throughout the novel. There are many different types of irony. Situational irony occurs when the opposite of what is expected happens. For example, Adam's father favors him over Charles, and Adam's life is difficult as a result. One might expect that Adam would not repeat this behavior, but he does by favoring his son Aron. This leads to tragedy in Adam's life.

In classical literature, tragic or dramatic irony occurs when the audience or reader knows something that a character does not. This knowledge is of something that will cause problems for the character. In *East of Eden*, the reader knows that Kate is an evil woman, yet Adam does not. The reader knows that Adam's relationship with her cannot possibly go well, given Kate's character and her past. As the story unfolds, Adam realizes her true nature.

Critical Responses

East of Eden quickly became a best seller, but overall, the critical response was not as positive as it had been for some of Steinbeck's earlier works. Some people thought that the subject matter was too large to tackle. Others did not like that the book was so different from the author's other books. Some critics objected to the characters, particularly that of Cathy, an unrealistic, extreme portrayal of a person with no redeeming qualities.[10] Steinbeck expected some negative responses. In a letter to his editor, Pascal Covici, he wrote: "You know as well as I do that this book is going to catch the same kind of hell that all the others did and for the same reasons. It will not be what anyone expects and so the expecters will not like it."[11]

The book has not become a classic in the sense that *Of Mice and Men* and *The Grapes of Wrath* have. In some ways, the book was forgotten, although it never went out of print. This is partly because many people think of his earlier works when they think of John

※エデンの東…それは青春の試練の園！

ジェームス・ディーン

エデンの東

This poster for the Japanese version of the movie *East of Eden* shows James Dean in the role of Cal Trask.

JOHN STEINBECK'S
EAST OF EDEN

Steinbeck. Nevertheless, literary scholars and critics have continued to read and analyze the novel since its publication.

East of Eden enjoyed a revival with the reading public in 2003 when Oprah Winfrey featured it in her book club. Her Web site featuring the book states this about the critics' responses:

> Despite the book's public popularity, literary critics remained extremely divided. In *John Steinbeck: A Biography,* author Jay Parini notes that in the *New York Times Book Review* Mark Schorer called *East of Eden* "probably the best of John Steinbeck's novels." Yet *Time* magazine dismissed the book as "a huge grab bag in which pointlessness and preposterous melodrama pop up frequently as good storytelling and plausible conduct."[12]

Steinbeck scholar John H. Timmerman states that Steinbeck had wanted to write about the Salinas Valley for years. While he used the setting in other works, *East of Eden* uses it most completely. The story also includes the author's personal views that are not as obvious in some other works. Timmerman writes: "*East of Eden* was to be the focal point for the moral views about humankind and human relationships that [Steinbeck] had been developing since his early thirties."[13] Regarding the critical response, Timmerman writes:

111

Despite the careful structuring and labor Steinbeck gave this work, it has met with little critical respect. Critics have objected to the presence of the first-person narrator as an intrusion. They have condemned the sprawling nature of the narrative.[14]

Not everyone agrees that the novel is weaker than his others, however. Another Steinbeck scholar, Robert DeMott, writes: "That book helped me identify the quality of Steinbeck's work I admired—his sense of story, family history, and oral tradition."[15] In an essay DeMott wrote about *East of Eden*, he praises Steinbeck's ability to evoke feelings in the reader, the narrator's soothing voice, and the author's adaptation of the Cain and Abel story.

Author Howard Levant writes in *The Novels of John Steinbeck:*

> The more balanced judgment is that *East of Eden* is a strangely unblended novel, an impressive, greatly flawed work, and a major summation of the various stresses between structure and materials which abound in Steinbeck's novels. The real importance of *East of Eden* does not lie in Steinbeck's mistaken claim to greatness, revealing as it is, but in its testimony—much like a completed blueprint—to the author's enduring difficulty in fusing structure and materials into a harmonious whole.[16]

112

Steinbeck's experimental use of form, structure, and content received mixed reviews. How did Steinbeck react to the first reviews? Biographer Jackson J. Benson writes:

> For the most part, the author was gratified with the reception the novel received, for although he disagreed with a number of things that were said and was hurt by a few others, he found that many of the reviews considered the book very carefully. By November *East of Eden* was number one on the fiction best-seller list—an event that may have caused some of the academic reviewers to lower their estimation of the novel."[17]

Chapter 7

Shelving Steinbeck: Challenges to His Books

> You might be shocked at the sensitive,
> controversial and inappropriate material that
> can be found in books in K-12 schools....
> Parents should be aware of what their chil-
> dren can or must read in school to decide
> whether it is appropriate for them or not....
> Bad is not for us to determine. Bad is what
> you determine is bad. Bad is what you think is
> bad for your child. What each parent consid-
> ers bad varies and depends on their unique
> situation, family and values. [1]

—Parents Against Bad Books in Schools

The three novels discussed here were not written for
children. They are for adult readers. The works
deal with some difficult issues, such as stereotypes,

prejudice, violence, and sexuality. Further, the novels use profanity and other terms that some consider offensive. Many people who argue that Steinbeck's works are not appropriate for high school classrooms believe that these issues and kinds of language are not suitable for young readers.

In recent years, most book challenges have been based on the books' lack of suitability for young readers. People ask to have books removed from classrooms and libraries because they are not age appropriate. Use of objectionable language, such as the language used in Steinbeck's books, is often believed to make a book inappropriate for younger readers.

Other reasons for wanting books removed often have to do with religious beliefs, particularly Christian beliefs. Steinbeck uses Christian themes throughout many of his books, but not always in a way that some Christians support. However, these concepts are not limited to Christianity. Ideas such as forgiveness, redemption, and love are universal themes that many people support. Many of the biblical themes are taken from the Old Testament, prior to Christ's birth. Some people appreciate the values represented in the books, while others are offended at the treatment of biblical themes and profanity, such as using "Jesus Christ" as a swear word.

Those who support the removal of such books often cite the First Amendment, which grants freedom of speech and freedom of religion. Those who oppose books based on their religious beliefs have a right to request educational materials that do not offend or go against their beliefs. Further, those who do not support certain books have as much freedom to say so as those who oppose censorship.

Racial issues are another reason Steinbeck's books are sometimes challenged. In *Of Mice and Men*, Crooks, the black stable hand, is referred to as a "nigger." The other characters' actions are racist, as they refuse Crooks a place to sleep in the bunkhouse. Instead, Crooks sleeps in a room attached to the barn, separate from the other men, like an animal. When Curley's wife threatens Crooks, he and the reader understand what she really means, even though she does not say it outright. If she said that Crooks made any sexual advances toward her, others would believe her because she is a white woman. The outcome for Crooks in such a situation, even if her claims were false, could be devastating.

Some readers find the blatant racism and use of racial epithets in the book to be highly offensive. Steinbeck himself was not trying to promote racism, but his characters use language he thought was accurate and portrayed the characters' racist viewpoints. Some people argue that Steinbeck was fighting racism by showing the ugliness of racial slurs. However, others argue that exposure to such terms can be harmful to African-American children, even if the author and the books are not racist. For example, in 1998, some parents wanted *Of Mice and Men* removed from the classrooms in a school in Oakley, California. Parents argued that other students learned and used racial slurs from the book.[2]

One argument in support of keeping books in the classroom is that teachers can guide students through discussions of the work. These difficult issues can be discussed in the open. Teachers can help students see other points of view. This process, they argue, helps students learn how to read objectively. It also helps them develop thinking skills necessary for drawing their own conclusions about the works. While this may be a strong argument, those who oppose certain books in the classroom can use this argument as well. They contend that it is possible to hold discussions of difficult issues using books that are not full of profanity; they say there are plenty of books that address social issues in a less controversial manner. Further, they argue, if students wish to read the controversial works, they can do so on their own time.

Nearly every school has some type of policy on which words are acceptable in school and which ones are not. Students can be suspended or even expelled for using words that are not acceptable. What happens when those words are in the texts that students study? In a typical classroom, teachers and students frequently read passages aloud from the works they are studying. Even when this is not the case, a thorough discussion of a work often requires students and teachers to use language from the books. This can create an awkward or embarrassing situation when the words in

117

the text are against the school's policy. One way to avoid this is to use works that do not contain those words.

Challenging Groups

Some organizations work to help parents and students challenge books that they feel are inappropriate for school use. Among them are Gateways to Better Education, the Family Research Council, and Family Friendly Libraries. These organizations support what they define as traditional family values and the freedom of religious expression in schools. This includes the freedom to refuse an assignment that goes against one's values or religion. Gateways to Education provides information on how to go about challenging a class-room book appropriately and legally. It stresses the need to follow the school's policy and provides support for those wishing to challenge a title.

Educational Research Analysts is an organization that reviews textbooks used in school curricula and rates them based on a number of categories. For literature, these categories include such issues as "amoral storylines, normalizing ethical cynicism and anti-social behavior, emphasis on death or sorrow, political correctness (e.g., anti-white, anti-male, anti-Christian bias), and editorial insensitivity (swearing, near-profanity, sexual suggestiveness)."[3] Other criteria include texts focused on death and dying, loneliness, and "whites as enemies and nonwhites as victims."[4] Clearly, Steinbeck's works are not appropriate based on a number of these

118

criteria, such as a focus on death and dying, and the treatment of minorities, women, and social outcasts.

People's reasons for wanting certain books banned from school use generally come from a desire to help or protect young readers. Whether an individual or group wants a book removed for its language or for racist themes, the underlying desire is often one of protecting youth. Some people believe that exposure to certain ideas, words, or concepts can be damaging. They want to ensure that students are old enough and mature enough to deal with these issues.

Reasons for Challenges

The American Library Association (ALA), which fights against book challenges and bans, provides a list of reasons for challenges between 1999 and 2000:

- 1,607 were challenges to "sexually explicit" material (up 161 since 1999);
- 1,427 to material considered to use "offensive language" (up 165 since 1999);
- 1,256 to material considered "unsuited to age group" (up 89 since 1999);
- 842 to material with an "occult theme or promoting the occult or Satanism," (up 69 since 1999);
- 737 to material considered to be "violent" (up 107 since 1999);
- 515 to material with a homosexual theme or "promoting homosexuality," (up 18 since 1999);

Sometimes objections to the content of books reaches an extreme point. In this photo, church members in Butler, Pennsylvania, burn books, CDs, and videos they believe are harmful to children.

- 419 to material "promoting a religious view point" (up 22 since 1999).

Other reasons for challenges included "nudity" (317 challenges, up 20 since 1999); "racism" (267 challenges, up 22 since 1999); "sex education" (224 challenges, up 7 since 1999); and "anti-family" (202 challenges, up 9 since 1999).[5]

Whether or not people agree with the reasoning, this list provides information about the concerns of people who challenge books. Many of these reasons relate directly to what is or is not appropriate for young readers. For those who wish to protect readers from such information, and for those whose personal beliefs are violated by such material, the issue is not simply freedom of speech or the freedom to read. It is a matter of maintaining personal moral standards and imparting those standards to one's children. Many parents wish to have some control over what their children read. Some students find these materials offensive as well. They have the right to refuse to read certain material based upon their values and beliefs.

The results of book challenges vary. Sometimes the removal of a book is successful, sometimes not. Overall, students often (but not always) have the option to choose an alternate assignment. For those who do not, organizations such as Gateways to Better Education help students work toward a solution.

Where do Steinbeck's books fall into the discussion? When his books are challenged, alternative texts include other Steinbeck books, such as *The Pearl*. This option may or may not be acceptable to the challenger. For those who have challenged Steinbeck's work in recent years, obscenity is the most common argument against the books.

When *Of Mice and Men* and *The Grapes of Wrath* were published, some of the initial concerns differed from the primary objections today. Steinbeck's language was targeted just as it has been more recently, but some of the first objections dealt with social issues. Some people felt that Steinbeck expressed anti-American sentiments. In his depiction of the state of migrant workers in *The Grapes of Wrath*, for example, he was criticized for portraying groups of people, such as California farmers, in a bad light. Some of the earlier censorship issues had as much to do with Steinbeck's social commentary as with the language he used.

Today, however, most of the concerns about Steinbeck's works have to do with the language and issues such as racism. *Of Mice and Men* uses the controversial racial slur "nigger" a number of times. This term was commonly used at the time of writing. Today, this is a highly charged, negative word. In some instances where the book has been challenged, racism and the use of that word are cited as examples why the book should not be used in the classroom. In a 1997 case in Sauk Rapids, Michigan, a student's mother complained that the book's racial epithets caused other students to harass her daughter. Although the mother challenged the book, the school superintendent chose to keep the book in use, arguing that the classroom was the most appropriate place to discuss issues of race.[6] In another 1997 case involving racism, the title was not removed, but students had the option to choose another assignment.[7]

Language in *Of Mice and Men* continues to be a troubling issue. In a 1999 case, Philip Ames, a parent, cited 173 profane words in the relatively short text. While the school board ultimately kept the book in the tenth-grade class, Ames is quoted as saying, "I'm disappointed when people in authority have a chance to make a decision to do something good for our children, but for the sake of literature, etc., they choose not to ruffle any feathers."[8]

Like *Of Mice and Men*, *The Grapes of Wrath* is challenged because of offensive language. The characters swear throughout the book, and even the character who used to be a preacher uses profanity. Casy, who still acts as a preacher from time to time (such as saying a prayer for Granma), is problematic for some people, particularly those with strong religious beliefs.

The book also deals with such controversial issues as violence and sexuality, which may be viewed as unsuitable for young readers. Some people object to Rose of Sharon's offering her breast milk to a dying man at the end of the story. For those who want to teach about social and historic issues, there are other books that deal with the Depression and the plight of migrant workers without using the type of language found in *The Grapes of Wrath*.

East of Eden, unlike the other two books, does not deal with migrant workers. It is a lengthy, in-depth look at two families. In addition to containing some offensive language, this novel, perhaps more so than the others, deals with a number of adult topics. The book's subject matter includes violence, sexuality, jealousy, broken families, and religion.

In 1982, high school libraries in Alabama and in Manitoba, Canada, removed *East of Eden*. Those who wanted the book removed considered it "ungodly and obscene."[9] However, *East of Eden* has not been challenged as much as *Of Mice and Men* and *The Grapes of Wrath* have, because books used in the classroom curriculum are more likely to be challenged than books that are just in the library or on supplemental reading lists. Students can choose to read a book from the library or on a list. In the classroom, however, students are expected to read materials required by the curriculum.

Chapter 8

In Steinbeck's Defense

> Intellectual freedom can exist only where two essential conditions are met: first, that all individuals have the right to hold any belief on any subject and to convey their ideas in any form they deem appropriate; and second, that society makes an equal commitment to the right of unrestricted access to information and ideas regardless of the communication medium used, the content of the work, and the viewpoints of both the author and receiver of information.[1]
>
> —American Library Association, *Intellectual Freedom Manual*

One reason Steinbeck's works are used in the classroom is that they can be used to study a number of different approaches to literature. The two works most often used in high school English classes are *Of Mice and Men* and *The Grapes of Wrath*. Many scholars consider both classic works in American literature. This reason alone makes them required reading for some students. Because these are the two Steinbeck novels most often used in schools, they are also the two works most often challenged. These works were not written for children or teens, but for adult readers. However, many American literary classics were written for adult audiences, and many classics are used in high school English classes. The concept of "children's books" developed during the twentieth century. Book designations such as "young adult" did not exist when Steinbeck wrote. Additionally, many high school courses (such as health classes) address adult issues. Classic pieces of literature have been used in high school curricula for many years. For some students, high school is the last time they are exposed to these classics, which is one reason why educators like to include them. Many classics portray a specific time in American or world history, and they allow students to study the relationship between societal events and literature.

There are many arguments for why Steinbeck's books should be used in the classroom or made available to students in the library. Some arguments have to do with reading rights in general. Others are specific to the work.

Of Mice and Men is used frequently in high school English classes. It is a study in form, writing style, societal values, and ethics, among other issues. The novel provides students an opportunity to discuss the story in terms of literary techniques, perspectives on history, and its place in American literature. Teachers and librarians can guide students through discussions of the work. When material is discussed openly, teachers can help students see different points of view. This process, they argue, helps students learn how to read objectively and to develop thinking skills necessary for drawing their own conclusions about the work.

A Right to Read?

Authors Ann K. Symons and Charles Harmon write in *Protecting the Right to Read*: "The idea that each and every citizen, regardless of status, education, or economic condition is entitled to free access to information is central to the library's mission."[2] They argue that libraries are important to protecting the First Amendment's guarantee of free speech: "After all, an author's right to write anything he or she wants to is meaningless if people don't have the freedom to read it."[3] They also state: "Libraries are forums for the free exchange of ideas and information. They provide a free people with the information they need to make informed choices. Libraries represent all points of view and, remarkably so for a publicly funded institution, are politically neutral."[4] In the case of public schools and public libraries, taxpayers' dollars provide the funding. Censorship and book challenging occur in both types of libraries.

Regarding school libraries, Symons and Harmon write: "One of the many methods that groups and individuals use to try to protect their children from harm is by attempting to control educational materials used in schools."[5] They argue that this practice goes against what the school system is designed to do—create an environment where students are exposed to different ideas and learn how to develop their own opinions. In other words, schools are one of the best places where students can learn to think freely and come up with ideas on their own. Teachers can instruct students in this process and provide multiple points of view to help students come to their own conclusions. When educational materials are limited for any reason, students are cheated out of this important learning opportunity.

In discussing censorship, Marjorie Heins writes in *Not in Front of the Children:* "Perhaps there are better ways to socialize children—among them, training in media literacy and critical thinking skills, comprehensive sexuality education, literature classes that *deal with* difficult topics rather than pretending they do not exist, and inclusion of young people in journalism and policy-making on this very issue."[6] She also argues that the only way students will learn to form their own opinions is by allowing them to do so. Restricting what students can or cannot learn only causes confusion and does not allow them to form their own thoughts on difficult subjects.

Censorship and book challenging in the schools are not new issues. In discussing the reasons why books were challenged between 1993 and 1994, Symons and

Harmon point out: "The most frequent complaints were about sexual content and objectionable language. The next most frequent category was against material at odds with the objector's religion."[7] More than a decade later, objectionable language continues to be a hot topic. Steinbeck's books are frequently challenged for this reason. Many of the reasons for book challenging have been similar over the past twenty-five years.

FREADOM

Celebrate
the right to read.

Banned Books Week
September 23-30, 2006

The American Library Association opposes efforts to censor library materials. Every year, the organization sponsors Banned Books Week, in support of the freedom to read.

Aside from its significance as one of Steinbeck's greatest novels, *The Grapes of Wrath* made history in another way. It led to the ALA's official position on censorship. When the book was banned throughout the country following publication, the association responded. The sixth edition of the ALA's *Intellectual Freedom Manual* states:

> The Association's basic position in opposition to censorship finally emerged in the late 1930s, when John Steinbeck's *The Grapes of Wrath* became the target of censorship pressures around the country. It was banned from libraries in East St. Louis, Illinois; Camden, New Jersey; Bakersfield, California; and other localities. While some objected to the "immorality" of the work, most opposed the social views advanced by the author.[8]

In 1939, the Association adopted the Library's Bill of Rights, followed by the creation of the Intellectual Freedom Committee, which advocates the ALA's goals of promoting free access to libraries and information.

In 1995, the ALA adopted a code of ethics. One of the items listed is "We uphold the principles of intellectual freedom and resist all efforts to censor library resources."[9] The ALA supports the efforts of all libraries, including public libraries and school libraries, to fight censorship and promote intellectual freedom.

Author Herbert N. Foerstel writes:

Of Mice and Men, published in 1937, has earned a host of awards while leaving a trail of controversy within the public school curriculum ... the censors claim to be protecting the young and impressionable from this tragic tale of crude heroes speaking vulgar language within a setting that implies criticism of our social system.[10]

Foerstel believes that the book remains a popular choice for teachers because it lends itself well to teaching. It is simple and clear, addressing difficult concepts and themes in an easy-to-understand format. The story "has plot structure uncluttered by diversions, distractions, or subplots, and its stark inevitability makes the point of the story unavoidable. The style is simple, using clear, direct sentences of description and action and the unadorned speech of simple people."[11] He argues that the story is a good lead-in to more difficult literary works such as the plays of Shakespeare.

There are a number of reasons that Steinbeck's work should be read in school. They are American classics. Steinbeck won the highest award for literature, the Nobel Prize. He continually experimented with his fiction. And he gave a voice to those people who did not have one.

Chapter 9

Steinbeck in the Twenty-first Century

Challenging, censoring, and banning books are not recent trends. Given the long history of censorship, it is not likely to go away. There will always be people who object to certain materials. As long as there is freedom of speech, there will be people who do not like what some others have to say. Censorship and book challenging in the school system are not new, either. Some individuals and groups will probably continue to challenge certain titles for years to come.

Although contemporary authors wrote many of the challenged titles in the past few years, Steinbeck's and others' titles will likely continue to face controversy. In recent years, challenges to Steinbeck books have continued, but they may be declining as other books enter the market. Overall, it seems that some authors are moving up on the list while Steinbeck moves down. One possible explanation is that in recent years,

This bust of John Steinbeck stands in Monterey, California, the site of many of his books. He is still honored as one of America's greatest writers.

publishers have shown more willingness to publish controversial books.

The ALA compiles annual lists of the most frequently challenged or banned books and their authors. An author may make the list of most frequently challenged even if a single book does not. This is because an author may have more than one challenged book. The individual titles do not make the list, but the total number of challenges places the author on the list. Steinbeck was often among the top ten in the early 2000s.[1] The most frequently challenged books are *Of Mice and Men* and *The Grapes of Wrath*. From 1990 to 2000, the ALA listed *Of Mice and Men* as number six out of the one hundred most frequently challenged books.[2] Over the years, Steinbeck's works have been banned or challenged for various reasons—and many of the early objections are similar to the reasons for challenging the books today. His works are regularly featured on the top one hundred banned books of all time. *The Grapes of Wrath* was the third most challenged book of the twentieth century, and *Of Mice and Men* was twelfth.[3] As of late 2006, *Of Mice and Men* was the fourth most challenged book of the twenty-first century.[4]

Steinbeck's books will likely continue to be challenged, even among controversial contemporary works. One reason is that his works are American literary classics. As a result, some teachers will want to use these books to teach about America's literary history—so they are more likely to appear in the curriculum and thus be subject to challenges. Also, even though society

134

is somewhat more tolerant of certain themes, ideas, or words than they were when the books were written, aspects of Steinbeck's books will continue to offend some people.

Changing Viewpoints

Which words are defined as profane or otherwise objectionable has changed somewhat over the past century, but not entirely. For instance, the word *damn* used to be highly offensive in everyday society, but it is now acceptable to some people. In recent years, terms such as *bitch* have also become more common, but it is still usually impolite to use the word, and it is a derogatory term when describing a person.

Much of the language in Steinbeck's books will continue to offend, even if more of the words gain acceptance. *Of Mice and Men* includes a wide range of profanity, so even if some terms become acceptable, others will not. Some of the words cross the line for acceptability because they refer to religious figures in a negative way. Racial terms will probably continue to be offensive, even if they are terms no longer generally used and even if they are considered in a historical context.

Whether young people should read or be exposed to the themes expressed in the books is a controversial topic in itself. Some people believe that every individual has the right to choose what he or she reads, even if that person is young. Others feel that young people need to be protected from reading such material until they are old enough to handle its themes and challenges. In many ways, the issue of book banning is not one of specific titles, but more about who decides what young people can or should read.

Why read Steinbeck? Perhaps Jeffrey Schultz and Luchen Li provide an answer when they write:

> In recent years, Steinbeck's reputation among scholars and critics has been redeemed. He has been identified as an early environmentalist, as a proto-feminist, as an advocate for social ethics, and as a proponent of cultural diversity. These labels are insufficient, yet they help outline the many aspects of Steinbeck's literary dimensions.[5]

Discussion Questions

1. Do you think young people need to be protected from some reading material? Why or why not?

2. Have you ever read a book that made you feel uncomfortable?

3. Who do you think should decide what books students read in school?

4. Do you support the idea of challenging or banning certain books? Why or why not?

5. Do you think Steinbeck's works should be used in schools? Why or why not?

339 B.C.E.—The philosopher Socrates is put to death for his works, which are judged to be disrespectful to the gods and corrupting to the young.

1450 C.E.—Gutenberg invents the printing press with movable type in Germany.

1791—The Bill of Rights (first ten amendments to the U.S. Constitution) is ratified.

1873—Comstock Law is passed, granting the authority to confiscate books thought to be "lewd, indecent, filthy or obscene."

1902—John Ernst Steinbeck is born on February 27 in Salinas, California.

1919—Steinbeck enters Stanford University.

1929—Steinbeck's first novel, *Cup of Gold*, is published.

1930—Steinbeck marries Carol Henning.

1936—Parts of the Comstock Law are declared unconstitutional.

1937—*Of Mice and Men* is published.

1939—*The Grapes of Wrath* is published.

1943—Steinbeck divorces Carol; later he marries Gwyndolyn Conger.

1944—The Steinbecks' son Thom is born.

1946—The Steinbecks' son John Steinbeck IV is born.

1948—John and Gwyndolyn are divorced.

1950—Steinbeck marries Elaine Anderson Scott.

1952—*East of Eden* is published.

1962—Steinbeck wins the Nobel Prize for Literature.

1964—Steinbeck receives the Medal of Freedom from President Lyndon Johnson.

1968—Steinbeck dies of heart disease.

1975—The Island Trees School District in Long Island, New York, removes nine books from the school library; students sue the school board in the U.S. District Court, claiming their First Amendment rights have been denied. They win.

1982—"Banned Books Week" is first celebrated nationally in the United States; held annually thereafter.

Chapter Notes

Chapter 1.
John Steinbeck: A History of Censorship

1. Nicholas J. Karolides, ed., *Banned Books: Literature Suppressed on Political Grounds* (New York: Facts On File, 1998), p. 222.

2. Ibid.

3. Ibid.

4. Ibid., pp. 222–223.

5. Ibid., p. 223.

6. Ibid., p. 224.

7. "Books Challenged/Banned in 2004–2005," Mountains & Plains Booksellers Association, n.d., <http://www.mountainsplains.org/censorship.html> (March 17, 2004).

8. "Vietnam Books, Steinbeck Banned by Mississippi High School," American Library Association, January 13, 2003, <http://www.ala.org/al_onlineTemplate.cfm?Section=january2003&Template=/ContentManagement/ContentDisplay.cfm&ContentID=12174> (March 17, 2006).

9. "Banned Books Week September 25 to October 2," University of California San Diego, 2000, <http://sshl.ucsd.edu/banned/books.html> (March 17, 2006).

Chapter 2.

Book Battles: Book Challenging, Book Banning, and Censorship

1. Jethro K. Lieberman, "Censorship," *World Book Online Reference Center,* 2006, <http://www.worldbookon line.com/wb/Article?id=ar102660> (February 4, 2006).

2. Ibid.

3. F. J. Church, trans., *Plato: Euthyphro, Apology, Crito,* The Library of Liberal Arts, Introduction by Robert D. Cumming (Upper Saddle River, N.J.: Prentice Hall, 1956), pp. viii–xv.

4. Marjorie Heins, *Not in Front of the Children* (New York: Hill and Wang, 2001), p. 5.

5. "BOARD OF EDUCATION v. PICO, 457 U.S. 853 (1982)," *Justia.com,* U.S. Supreme Court Center, <http:// supreme.justia.com/us/457/853/case.html#F7> (December 18, 2006).

6. "Board of Education v. Pico," 457 U.S. 853 (1982), Docket Number: 80–2043, Abstract, Oyez, U.S. Supreme Court Multimedia, 1996–2005, <http://www.oyez.org/ oyez/resource/case/1060/> (February 16, 2006).

7. Ibid.

8. "The Most Frequently Challenged Books of 1990–2000," American Library Association, n.d., <www.ala.org/ala/oif/bannedbooksweek/bbwlink/100 mostfrequently.htm> (February 8, 2005).

9. Claire Mullally, "Banned Books: Overview," First Amendment Center, February 9, 2006, <http://www.first

amendmentcenter.org/Speech/libraries/topic.aspx? topic=banned_books> (February 16, 2006).

10. Nicholas J. Karolides, ed., *Banned Books: Literature Suppressed on Political Grounds* (New York: Facts On File, 1998), p. vii.

11. *Merriam-Webster Online*, 2005–2006, <http: //www.webster.com/cgi-bin/dictionary?va= vulgar> (February 16, 2006).

12. Herbert N. Foerstel, *Banned in the U.S.A.* (Westport, Conn.: Greenwood Press, 2002), p. xii.

13. Diane Ravitch, *The Language Police* (New York: Alfred A. Knopf, 2003), pp. 3–30ff.

14. Ibid., p. 115.

15. Ibid.

16. Ibid., p. 25.

17. Eric Buehrer, "Challenging a Book in Your School," Gateways to Better Education, 1998, <http://www.gtbe.org/news/index.php/1/14/35.html> (March 6, 2006).

18. "By the Book/Understanding the Proper Process for Removing a Book," Gateways to Better Education, 2000, <http://www.gtbe.org/news/index.php/1/14/36.h tml> (March 6, 2006).

19. Marjorie Heins, *Not in Front of the Children* (New York: Hill and Wang, 2001), p. 5.

Chapter 3.

Steinbeck: A Life in Search of Truth

1. Jackson J. Benson, *John Steinbeck, Writer* (New York: Penguin Books, 1984), p. 19.

2. Ibid., p. 587.

3. Ibid., pp. 19–21.

4. John Steinbeck, *Sea of Cortez*, taken from *The Portable Steinbeck*, ed. Pascal Covici, Jr. (New York: Penguin Books, 1976), p. 485.

5. Jeffrey Schultz and Luchen Li, *Critical Companion to John Steinbeck: A Literary Reference to His Life and Work* (New York: Facts On File, 2005), p. 308.

6. Benson, p.369.

7. Ibid., p. 586.

8. Schultz and Li, p. 12.

9. Ibid., p. 15.

10. "John Steinbeck, The Nobel Prize in Literature 1962, Banquet Speech," Nobelprize.org, 1962, <http://nobelprize.org/nobel_prizes/literature/laureates/1962/steinbeck-speech.html> (December 18, 2006).

11. Ibid.

12. Schultz and Li, p. 15.

13. Benson, p. 1038.

Chapter 4.

Of Mice and Men

1. Jeffrey Schultz and Luchen Li, *Critical Companion to John Steinbeck: A Literary Reference to His Life and Work* (New York: Facts On File, 2005), p. 145.

2. John Steinbeck, *Of Mice and Men*, taken from *The Portable Steinbeck*, ed. Pascal Covici, Jr. (New York: Penguin Books, 1976), p. 261.

3. Ibid., p. 322.

4. Ibid., p. 296.

5. Ibid., p. 282.

6. William Goldhurst, "A Parable of the Curse of Cain," in *Literary Companion Series, John Steinbeck: Of Mice and Men*, Jill Karson, ed. (San Diego: Greenhaven Press, 1998), p. 48.

7. Ibid., p. 52.

8. Lee Dacus, "Lennie as Christian in *Of Mice and Men*," *Southwestern American Literature*, vol. 4, 1974, pp. 87–91.

9. Schultz and Li, p. 146.

10. Mark Van Doren, "*Of Mice and Men* by John Steinbeck," book review, *Nation*, March 6, 1937, p. 275.

11. John H. Timmerman, *John Steinbeck's Fiction: The Aesthetics of the Road Taken* (Norman, Okla.: University of Oklahoma Press, 1986), p. 97.

12. Ibid.

13. Lee Dacus, "Christian Symbolism in Of Mice and Men," in *Literary Companion Series, John Steinbeck: Of Mice and Men*, Jill Karson, ed. (San Diego: Greenhaven Press, 1998), pp. 80–85.

14. Ibid., p. 80.

15. Ibid., pp. 83–85.

16. Schultz and Li, p. 147.

17. Van Doren.

18. R. Ganapathy, "Steinbeck's *Of Mice and Men*: A Study of Lyricism Through Primitivism," *Literary Criterion*, vol. 5, no. 3, Winter 1962.

19. Ibid.

20. Richard Astro, *John Steinbeck and Edward F. Ricketts: The Shaping of a Novelist* (Minneapolis, Minn.: University of Minnesota Press, 1973), p. 105.

21. Ibid.

22. Harry Thornton Moore, *The Novels of John Steinbeck: A First Critical Study* (Chicago: Normandie House, 1939), unpaged.

23. Ibid.

24. Schultz and Li, p. 148.

Chapter 5.
The Grapes of Wrath

1. John Steinbeck, *The Grapes of Wrath* (New York: Penguin Books, 1999), p. 381.

2. Ibid., p. 214.

3. Ibid., pp. 169–170.

4. Anne Lyon Haight, *Banned Books: Informal Notes on Some Books Banned for Various Reasons at Various Times and in Various Places* (New York: R. R. Bowker Company, 1970), p. 93.

5. Lee Burress, University of Wisconsin-Stevens Point, "*The Grapes of Wrath*: Preserving Its Place in the Curriculum," *Celebrating Censored Books*, eds. Nicholas J. Karolides and Lee Burress (Racine, Wis.: Wisconsin Council of Teachers of English, 1985), p. 53.

6. Steinbeck, p. 365.

7. Haight, p. 93.

8. Jeffrey Schultz and Luchen Li, *Critical Companion to John Steinbeck: A Literary Reference to His Life and Work* (New York: Facts on File, 2005), p. 90.

9. J. P. Hunter, "Steinbeck's Wine of Affirmation in *The Grapes of Wrath*," *Essays in Modern Literature* (DeLand, Fla.: Stetson University Press, 1963), unpaged.

10. Ibid.

11. Ibid.

12. Ibid.

13. B. R. McElderry, Jr., "*The Grapes of Wrath*: In the Light of Modern Critical Theory," in *A Companion to The Grapes of Wrath*, ed. Warren French (New York: Viking Press, 1972), p. 208.

14. Schultz and Li, p. 102.

Chapter 6.
East of Eden

1. John Steinbeck, *East of Eden*, 2002 ed. (New York: Penguin Books, 1952), p. 299.

2. Ibid.

3. Ibid., p. 3.

4. Jeffrey Schultz and Luchen Li, *Critical Companion to John Steinbeck: A Literary Reference to His Life and Work* (New York: Facts On File, 2005), p. 73.

5. Genesis 3:23, *Good News Bible: The Bible in Today's English Version* (New York: American Bible Society, 1976).

6. Ibid., 3:24.

7. Ibid., 4:16.

8. Genesis 4:16, *Holy Bible: Old and New Testaments in the King James Version* (Burlington, Ontario: Inspirational Promotions, n.d).

9. Schultz and Li, p. 73.

10. Ibid.

11. "THE NOVEL: Steinbeck Catches Critical Hell," Oprah's Book Club, 2006, <http://www.oprah.com/obc_classic/featbook/eastofeden/novel/eoe_novel_critics.jhtml> March 21, 2006.

12. Ibid.

13. John H. Timmerman, *John Steinbeck's Fiction* (Norman, Okla.: University of Oklahoma Press, 1986), p. 212.

14. Ibid., p. 215.

15. Robert DeMott, "Of Ink and Heart's Blood," in *John Steinbeck: A Centennial Tribute*, ed. Stephen K. George (Westport: Conn.: Praeger, 2002), p. 126.

16. Howard Levant, *The Novels of John Steinbeck* (Columbia, Mo.: University of Missouri Press, 1974), p. 234.

17. Jackson J. Benson, *John Steinbeck, Writer* (New York: Penguin Books, 1984), p. 732.

Chapter 7.
Shelving Steinbeck: Challenges to His Books

1. "Welcome," Parents Against Bad Books in Schools (PABBIS), n.d., <http://www.pabbis.com> (December 26, 2006).

2. Herbert N. Foerstel, *Banned in the U.S.A.* (Westport, Conn.: Greenwood Press, 2002), p. 200.

3. "2001 Grades 7–8 Literature Textbook Ratings," Educational Research Analysts, 2001, <http://www.textbookreviews.org/pdf/sample_amlit-wohist_review_criteria.pdf> (May 11, 2007).

4. "High School Literature," Educational Research Analysts, 2000, <http://www.textbookreviews.org/pdf/2001_elsci-hslit_ratings.pdf> (May 11, 2007).

5. American Library Association, "Challenged and Banned Books," 2006, <http://www.ala.org/ala/

oif/bannedbooksweek/challengedbanned/challenged banned.htm> (March 18, 2006).

6. Foerstel, p. 199.

7. Ibid., pp. 199–200.

8. Ibid., p. 200.

9. "Censored Books in the USA," 1994/1996, <http://home.nvg.org/~aga/bulletin43.html, (March 18, 2006).

Chapter 8.
In Steinbeck's Defense

1. American Library Association, *Intellectual Freedom Manual*, sixth ed. (Chicago: Office for Intellectual Freedom of the American Library Association, 2002), p. xiii.

2. Ann K. Symons and Charles Harmon, *Protecting the Right to Read* (New York: Neal-Schuman Publishers, 1995), p. 2.

3. Ibid., p. 1.

4. Ibid., p. 2.

5. Ibid., pp. 52–53.

6. Marjorie Heins, *Not in Front of the Children* (New York: Hill and Wang, 2001), p. 11.

7. Symons and Harmon, p. 53.

8. American Library Association, p. 7.

9. American Library Association, "Code of Ethics of the American Library Association, adopted June 28,

1995," 2005, <http://www.ala.org/ala/oif/statements pols/codeofethics/codeethics.htm> (March 22, 2006).

10. Herbert N. Foerstel, *Banned in the U.S.A.* (Westport, Conn.: Greenwood Press, 2002), pp. 197–198.

11. Ibid., p. 198.

Chapter 9.
Steinbeck in the Twenty-first Century

1. American Library Association, "Challenged and Banned Books," 2006, <http://www.ala.org/ala/oif/ bannedbooksweek/challengedbanned/challenge banned.htm> (March 16, 2006).

2. American Library Association, "The 100 Most Frequently Challenged Books of 1990–2000," 2005, <http://www.ala.org/ala/oif/bannedbooksweek/bbwlink s/top100.pdf> (March 16, 2006).

3. American Library Association, "Banned and/or Challenged Books from the Radcliffe Publishing Course Top 100 Novels of the 20th Century," 2005, <http://www.ala.org/ala/pio/piopresskits/bbbwpresskit/ bannedchallenged.htm> (December 18, 2006).

4. American Library Association, "Most Challenged Books of 21st Century (2000–2005)," 2006, <http://www.ala.org/ala/oif/bannedbooksweek/bbwlink s/topten2000to2005.htm> (December 18, 2006).

5. Jeffrey Schultz and Luchen Li, *Critical Companion to John Steinbeck: A Literary Reference to His Life and Work* (New York: Facts On File, 2005), p. 17.

Published works of John Steinbeck

Books

<table>
<tr><td>1957</td><td>*The Short Reign of Pippin IV*</td></tr>
<tr><td>1958</td><td>*Once There Was a War*</td></tr>
<tr><td>1961</td><td>*The Winter of Our Discontent*</td></tr>
<tr><td>1962</td><td>*Travels With Charley: In Search of America*</td></tr>
<tr><td>1966</td><td>*America and Americans*</td></tr>
<tr><td>1969</td><td>*Journal of a Novel: The East of Eden Letters*</td></tr>
<tr><td>1975</td><td>*Steinbeck: A Life in Letters*</td></tr>
<tr><td>1975</td><td>*Viva Zapata!*</td></tr>
<tr><td>1976</td><td>*The Acts of King Arthur and His Noble Knights*</td></tr>
<tr><td>1978</td><td>*Letters to Elizabeth*</td></tr>
<tr><td>1986</td><td>*Uncollected Stories of John Steinbeck*</td></tr>
<tr><td>1989</td><td>*Working Days: The Journals of The Grapes of Wrath*</td></tr>
</table>

Plays

<table>
<tr><td>1937</td><td>*Of Mice and Men*</td></tr>
<tr><td>1942</td><td>*The Moon Is Down*</td></tr>
<tr><td>1950</td><td>*Burning Bright*</td></tr>
</table>

Screenplays

<table>
<tr><td>1941</td><td>*The Forgotten Village*</td></tr>
<tr><td>1944</td><td>*Lifeboat*</td></tr>
<tr><td>1945</td><td>*A Medal for Benny*</td></tr>
<tr><td>1948</td><td>*The Pearl*</td></tr>
<tr><td>1949</td><td>*The Red Pony*</td></tr>
<tr><td>1952</td><td>*Viva Zapata!*</td></tr>
</table>

Glossary

American Library Association (ALA)—A professional organization supporting libraries and librarians. The ALA is against censorship and book banning.

backstory—The parts of a story that take place before the current telling of the story.

bindle stiff—A migrant worker, typically from the 1930s, who did not have a permanent home and traveled from one job to another.

censorship—The practice of keeping information from a group of people. This can happen on a large scale, such as a government's banning a book, or in a smaller setting, such as in a school.

derogatory—A term or action that expresses a low opinion of someone or something.

Dust Bowl—An area of the United States that suffered extreme drought during the 1930s, leading to large dust clouds over several southwestern and midwestern states.

epithet—Rude or disparaging term referring to a person or group of people.

First Amendment—Part of the American Constitution's Bill of Rights that guarantees freedom of speech and freedom of religious expression.

free speech—The ability to speak about anything within the context of the law, as protected by the First Amendment. The law prohibits certain types of speech, such as defamatory, treasonable, or obscene speech.

Great Depression—A period of great poverty in America following the stock market crash in 1929 and continuing until World War II in the early 1940s.

literary device—An aspect of literature that is used to create a work, such as plot, setting, characterization, etc.

migrant workers—Workers who travel from one job to another.

Nobel Prize—An international award given yearly since 1901 for achievements in physics, chemistry, medicine, literature, and for peace.

phalanx theory—Steinbeck's view that individuals make up a larger organism, which has a life of its own.

plot—The main story line of a novel or piece of fiction.

point of view—How an author chooses to tell a story. The most common types are first person, where an individual tells a story, and third person, where a narrator tells the story.

propaganda—Material used to promote one point of view and downplay another.

Glossary

racism—A belief that race creates certain human characteristics and that some races are better or worse than others are.

setting—Where and when a story takes place.

symbolism—The use of ideas, words, or things to represent an idea or belief.

teleological theory—A view examining the reasons why events occur in the lives of animals and people.

Bloom, Harold, editor. *John Steinbeck's Of Mice and Men*. Philadelphia: Chelsea House, 2006.

Farish, Leah. *The First Amendment: Freedom of Speech, Religion and the Press*. Berkeley Heights, N.J.: Enslow Publishers, 1998.

Heavilin, Barbara A., editor. *The Critical Response to John Steinbeck's The Grapes of Wrath*. Westport, Conn.: Greenwood Press, 2000.

Karolides, Nicholas J., Margaret Bald, and Dawn Sova. *100 Banned Books: Censorship Histories of World Literature*. New York: Checkmark Books/Facts On File, 1999.

Newman, Gerald, and Eleanor Newman Layfield. *A Student's Guide to John Steinbeck*. Berkeley Heights, N.J.: Enslow Publishers, Inc., 2004.

Ravitch, Diane. *The Language Police: How Pressure Groups Restrict What Students Learn*. New York: Knopf, 2003.

Tessitore, John. *John Steinbeck: A Writer's Life*. New York: Franklin Watts, 2001.

Tracy, Kathleen. *John Steinbeck*. Hockessin, Del.: Mitchell Lane Publishers, 2005.

Internet Addresses

Anti-Banning Site:

The American Library Association

\<http://www.ala.org\>

Pro-Challenging Site:

Family Research Council

\<http://www.frc.org\>

The National Steinbeck Center

\<http://www.steinbeck.org\>

Index